Aug 1991

To A True Friend
& Avid collector
Happy Birthday —

# DECORATIVE GOLF COLLECTIBLES

## COLLECTOR'S INFORMATION
## CURRENT PRICES

### BY SHIRLEY & JERRY SPRUNG

### EDITED BY: BETH KIRSNER

PUBLISHED BY: GARY KIRSNER
GLENTIQUES, LTD., CORAL SPRINGS, FLORIDA

While every care has been taken in compiling the information contained in this volume, neither the authors, the editor nor the publisher can accept any liablity for loss, financial or otherwise, incurred by reliance placed on the information herein.

**Cataloging in Publication Data**

Sprung, Shirley, 1935-
    Decorative golf collectibles : collector's information, current
prices / by Shirley & Jerry Sprung. --
    p.  cm.
    Includes bibliographical references and index.
    ISBN 0-9614130-4-2
    ISBN 0-9614130-5-0 (pbk.)

    1. Golf--Collectibles--Catalogs.   2. Golf--Collectors and
collecting.   I. Sprung, Jerry, 1932-  II. Title.

GV979.C6                    796.352
                            QBI91 - 170

Published by Glentiques, Ltd.
P.O. Box 8807
Coral Springs, FL 33075
Telephone: (305) 344-9856
FAX: (305) 344-4421

Printed in the United States of America
Printed by: Walsworth Publishing
Color Separations by: Rex Three, Inc.

# CONTENTS

**AKNOWLEDGEMENTS**

This book would not have been possible without thc generous help of many collectors and antique dealers. We would like to thank Barbara & Mel Alpren, David Berkowitz of Golf's Golden Years, Lee & Harold Berman, Joan & Sidney Cohen, Graham Dry, Steve Gelfand, Diane Goedkoop, Louise Irvine, Peter Kassai, Mary & Walter Kraus, John Macyshyn, Irving Miller, Richard Morchan, Mimi Rudnick, Lowell Schulman, Jerri Schwartz, and Roberta & William Willner.

# PREFACE

We are collectors.

About twenty-five years ago, we started our first serious collection. We had been collecting one thing or another for years before that, including cut glass, cloisonné, tooth pick holders, and nineteenth century sterling silver. In many cases our collections just grew and when we had an interesting assortment, we stopped. These collections were put together on a whim. They had no firm place in our lives and we never stopped to research them or join collector organizations relating to them.

That changed when photographic collecting became part of our lives. Photography had always been important to us, as had antiques. My wife, Shirley, would drag me through endless antique shows and flea markets (despite my occasional protests). But one day, as patience was running low, she pointed to a counter full of old cameras. I had some knowledge of contemporary and pre-WWII photography equipment and started to collect the items I remembered from my youth. We bought everything in sight, primarily at prices ranging from $5.00 to $25.00.

One day we were offered a unique camera at a cost of $2000.00. That purchase represented a turning point in our lives as collectors. We realized we needed more knowledge to make decisions involving relatively more expensive purchases. We joined historical societies where we met other collectors, authors, and historians in the field. Eventually I became president of the largest historical society in the country, the American Photographic Collectors Society. Thus, we met many other collectors, and expanded our understanding of the history behind our collection enormously. We viewed collections all over the United States and Europe, and we studied the philosophies of the collectors.

About a year before we disposed of our photography collection, some golfing friends showed us several lovely golf collectibles they had found at antique shows, and the bug bit again. Shirley and I found a rusty old wooden shaft putter, which marked the start of our latest collection. We advised our friends that cameras were "out" and golf was "in". We joined the Golf Collector's Society of America, attended several auctions, and started to meet other collectors. We found that golf collecting included a number of specialties, such as old golf clubs and balls, catalogs, patented devices, books, and items of all kinds decorated with a golf scene or motif. We decided that our knowledge lent itself best to the last category, and made that our specialty.

As our collection grew, we photographed each item we bought. We eventually put the photos in an album, which we used to show dealers what we had and what we were seeking.

The album grew and we took it to the collectors meetings and golf auctions. It was a wonderful tool in comparing notes with other collectors. We made many new friends from all over the United States and Europe, just as we had through our previous collection.

The pleasure we and others derive from sharing the photographs of our golf collection led to the decision to share them with you here in **Decorative Golf Collectibles**. The following pages testify to our efforts and those of our fellow collectors, David Berkowitz, and Lowell Schulman.

Many people have asked us about our success in the collecting field, and we thought that a few pointers would be useful to beginning and veteran collectors alike.

- We never start collecting anything with the idea that it will be an investment.
- We never buy anything because it is cheap.
- We never sacrifice quality for quantity.
- Serious collections are in fields about which we are both knowledgeable and passionate.
- We only buy objects which are aesthetically pleasing to us.
- One of the most important collections we have is people: other collectors, writers, historians, and dealers.
- We try to remember the circumstances involved in obtaining pieces. These stories are a part of our lives and a source of endless enjoyment.
- We rejoice in the triumphs of other collectors, and never feel jealous of them.
- We are pleased to share our knowledge with others, and hope they will do the same with us. We are rarely disappointed!

*Dedicated to Sara & Daniel,*
*"Our finest collection"*

# INTRODUCTION

Collecting is a reflection of the personality or interests of the collector. Whether it be jewelry, automobiles, art glass, baseball cards or any one of thousands of other collecting categories, there must be a tie between the collector and the objects being collected.

Collectibles can range from oil paintings by the masters, fetching millions of dollars, to very recently produced figurines selling for under twenty dollars. An interest in collecting can be generated by artistic merit, or an investment strategy.

Collecting is a centuries old endeavor and is now popular around the world. Most collections focus on either the products of a certain material, such as glass or silver, or a category such as toys or beer steins. In recent years collectors have begun to focus on many topical areas such as baseball, bicycles, aviation, and of course, golf.

Golf collecting has existed for many years, and has long been concentrated in the areas of golf balls, golf clubs and golfing literature. In recent years, wide interest has developed in collecting decorative golf collectibles made from ceramics, glass, silver and other materials.

Growth of interest in golf as a sport has led to a corresponding growth in the interest of collectors. Naturally, as there has been an increase in the number of collectors of golfing items, prices have increased. In the last few years, the value of most pre-1940 golf motif collectibles has increased such that they command a large premium over similar items with non-golf decorations.

Many collectibles have experienced price increases greater than the rate of inflation over the last decade, some at a staggering rate. Included in this group are many of the decorative golf collectibles featured in this book. The value of many of these items has increased by more than 300% over the last 10 years. As is the case with most collectibles, the items with the greatest inherent quality have been the most sought after, and therefore have increased in value at the highest rate.

Values indicated following the descriptions of items in this book are based on the sale of the same or similar items at auctions in the United States and Great Britain, as well as numerous private transactions.

# CERAMICS

The most popular materials in which we find golf motif collectibles are ceramics. The family of ceramic golf items includes stoneware, earthenware and porcelain.

## MATERIALS

The terms used to describe ceramics can be confusing. The use of color as a distinguishing factor is limited, as porcelain is opaque white, and earthenware is usually tan, but stoneware can be tan or gray. Further confusion comes from use of the word "pottery", which can refer to any of these materials when talking about American ceramics, though it most often refers to stoneware. This usage originated with the description of decorative American ceramics as "art pottery".

**Stoneware** is vitrified (melted and solidified) clay, fired at a temperature of 1200° to 1300° C. It is very hard and non-porous, making it impervious to liquids. Stoneware is frequently decorated with a saltglaze, achieved by throwing salt into the kiln when the highest temperature is reached during the firing, producing a thin and very hard glaze.

**Earthenware** differs from stoneware in several ways. The earthenware vessel, fired at a relatively low temperature of no more than 1200° C, does not vitrify and retains a porous texture. Glaze applied to earthenware remains as a surface layer, as opposed to stoneware, in which glaze fuses to the clay body. Earthenware requires a glaze finish to be used as a vessel to hold liquid.

**Porcelain,** on the other hand, is more similar to stoneware. It is comprised of kaolin (china clay) and pentunse (china stone), which are the names for various stages in the decomposition of granite. Also known as bone china, it is about one-quarter kaolin, one-quarter pentunse and one-half powdered bone of oxen or cattle. Porcelain is fired to vitrification at about 1350°, and as with stoneware, glazes become fused with the porcelain body.

1.    Three handled loving cup, 5½" h., porcelain, hand painted, made by Ceramic Art Company (see page 13), c.1900, $6000-9000.

Because of their respective compositions and the way in which the materials are typically utilized, there are variations in their susceptibility to damage. Porcelain is often used in the production of plates and figurines with relatively thin areas such as the rim or appendages. While porcelain is an extremely hard material, its use in this manner leaves it quite vulnerable to chipping. Earthenware is also frequently designed in ways that make it likely to incur some damage if more than the mildest impact occurs. Stoneware, on the other hand, is much less likely to break thanks to typically thicker designs and rounded edges.

## DECORATION

Color plays an important role in the decorative value of ceramic golf collectibles. There are a variety of means of decorating ceramics, many of which are demonstrated in the golf scenes viewed on the following pages.

When a ceramic object requires color over the entire piece, it can be achieved in two ways. Traces of various metals are found in the clays used in ceramics, and these impart a natural color to the object, such as the familiar red of most clay which comes from the presence of iron. Clay with other metallic "impurities", either naturally present or purposefully added,

will show a range of resulting colors. While the color of stoneware or earthenware objects is often determined by the presence of trace metals, porcelain is more often, though not exclusively, produced in its white translucent form and colored with a glaze.

Glazes are another method of achieving the desired overall color in a ceramic object, as well as adding gloss to an otherwise matte finished surface. Glaze consists of silica (a hard, glassy mineral) and one or more fluxes (materials which promote fusion of metals or minerals by lowering their melting point). To these ingredients, one would add various metal oxides to achieve the desired color or effect. The presence of copper imparts green shades to the glaze, while cobalt provides blue and tin produces an opaque white glaze. Combinations of various metallic oxides produce many more gradations of color. For instance, a relatively deep shade of brownish purple is achieved by introducing impure manganese ore, but purified manganese gives softer brown and purple shades, while the presence of iron in conjunction with manganese produces black.

While colored glazes are useful in a protective as well as a decorative sense, more detailed and localized designs may be applied to ceramics by several methods, and may be done in conjunction with glazing as described above.

2. Vases, 11"h., porcelain, hand painted, one vase signed P. Mitchell 1910, titled *Through the Green*, and *The Drive Off*, expensive.

Enamel is a popular form of decoration on ceramics, as well as on other materials, such as may be seen in the chapters of this book covering silver and glass. Enamel is a glass compound with a large proportion of lead or other flux. The flux brings the material to the low melting point necessary to enable it to fuse with the already fired ceramic body (whether glazed or not) in a relatively low-temperature muffle kiln. Muffle firing is used to protect the ceramic wares from the main heat of the kiln by placing them behind *muffling* fire bricks. This preserves the purity of the enamel colors, which could not be maintained at higher temperatures.

Glaze and enamel decorations are the most popular methods for coloring and decorating golf motif ceramics. But there are other methods of achieving dramatic decorative effects.

Slip is the name for clay thinned with water, which has a number of uses in ceramic decoration, as well as in the assembly of molded pieces. Engobe is the process of coating the ceramic body with slip to conceal its natural color, in preparation for either sgraffito or incising. Sgraffito is the method of scratching a decoration through the top layer to the underlying color, whereas incising is shallow and does not show the underlying color.

In addition to the attributes of color that slip can provide, it is also useful in creating raised or impressed designs. Slip casting is a method of molding which imparts precise detail on a relatively thin ceramic body. A plaster of paris mold with the desired pattern on its interior absorbs the water from slip poured into it. Done repeatedly, the remaining clay reflects the pattern of the mold once the mold is removed.

3.    Figurine, 6³/4" h., porcelain, made by Robj, golf bag holds 8 chrome golf club stirrers, 1920's, $1000-1400.

4.    Cocktail shaker, 11" h., porcelain, made by Robj, removable hat with cork stopper, removable head for pouring, 1920's, $1500-2000.

**Robj** was a Parisian porcelain dealer during the 1920's, and sponsored annual design competitions, some of whose winners' designs were produced by Robj's Sèvres factory in limited editions. Figural objects such as the drinking accessories above were typical Robj products, as were desk and smoking items. Robj went out of business in the early 1930's.

Robj

Paris

Molding itself, whether performed using liquid slip or malleable clay is the most common method of forming a ceramic vessel or figure. Because the process makes it easy to produce multiple copies of identical items, molding is the most practical method of manufacturing more than very limited editions of an item. Molds can be designed in one or several parts, with a raised intaglio design which impresses a decoration into the material, or a recessed decoration into which the material flows to create a relief design.

Finally, a colored decoration may be achieved by use of transfer printing. This is also a method conducive to mass production, in that a thin piece of paper is imprinted with a design in enamel, which is then transferred to the ceramic body and fired to fuse the design to the underlying glaze.

## COLLECTING

Most of the items shown on the following pages could be considered production items, of which relatively large quantities *may* have been made. Where reference is made to hand painting or signed pieces, the quantities to be found will be significantly lower.

The potential for reproductions, fakes, or newly created items which can confuse collectors definitely exists in the area of ceramic golf art. The highest risk is run in the area of simply shaped items, such as plates, whose transfer decorations are easily duplicated using the same technology used to create the originals.

5.   Vase, 19" h., porcelain, hand painted, made by Sèvres (the French national porcelain manufacturer), signed M. Herbillon, dated 1939, expensive.

6.   Pitcher, 14½" h., porcelain, hand painted, made by Ceramic Art Company, c.1900, $6000-9000.

Fortunately, reproduction of ceramic golf art has not yet become a problem. However, there is risk in ignoring the visible warning signs, including lack of a recognized manufacturer's mark, an unrecognizable overall design, or modern clothing styles. If you don't recognize the design itself, even more careful attention should be paid to the marks than usual. Be aware, however, that the marks shown with factory information will be present on some of that manufacturer's products, but usually not on all of them.

The manufacturers of the various ceramic golf collectibles were predominantly English, led by Royal Doulton, in Lambeth and later in Burslem. In fact, most of the English manufacturers of

ceramic golf collectibles were concentrated in the Stoke-on-Trent area of the Staffordshire region. A few American manufacturers followed with fairly substantial quantities of golf motif ceramics, while Germany and Austria contributed smaller quantities. Other countries accounted for only a handful of items. The quantity of golf collectibles produced in each country related closely to the popularity of the game in that country at the time.

The majority of ceramic golf art is functional, and often served a purpose related to smoking or drinking. There are, however, large numbers of purely decorative golf ceramics, including figurines, vases and wall plaques.

7, 8 and 10. Three beer mugs, ½ liter, porcelain, made by Ceramic Art Company, similar scenes, but variations exist due to hand-painting, c.1900, $2000-2500.

9. Toothpick holder, 2 3/4" h., porcelain with beaded silver rim, hand painted, made by Ceramic Art Company, c.1900, $1000-1500.

Walter Scott Lenox founded the **Ceramic Art Company** in Trenton, New Jersey in 1889 as a partnership, but Lenox assumed complete control around 1895. In 1906, the name was changed to Lenox China Company. Known for strict quality control, Lenox has produced both porcelain tableware and giftware, and presently the name encompasses a group of several porcelain and glass manufacturers.

11.   Three handled loving cup, 4" h., porcelain with silver rim, hand painted, made by Ceramic Art Company (see page 13), c.1900, $4000-6000.

12.   Beer mug, ½ liter, porcelain with gold washed rim, hand painted, made by Ceramic Art Company (see page 13), c.1900, $2000-2500.

13.   Jug, 5 ¾" h., porcelain with gold wash inside lip, hand painted, made by Ceramic Art Company for O'Hara Dial Co., early 1900's, $4000-6000.

14.   Beer stein, no lid, ½ liter, porcelain, hand painted, made by Royal Bonn (see page 19), late 1800's, $2500-3500.

15.   Beer stein, ½ liter, porcelain with silver lid, hand painted, made by Ceramic Art Company (see page 13), Horace Hutchinson pictured, c.1900, $2500-3500.

16.   Beer stein, ½ liter, porcelain with silver lid, hand painted, made by Ceramic Art Company (see page 13), c.1900, $2500-3500.

17. Beer stein, ⁴/₁₀ liter, porcelain with inlaid lid, hand painted, made by Ceramic Art Company for O'Hara Dial Co., early 1900's, $2000-2500.

18. Beer stein, ½ liter, porcelain with inlaid lid, hand painted, made by Ceramic Art Company for O'Hara Dial Co., early 1900's, $2000-2500.

19. Beer stein, ⁴/₁₀ liter, porcelain with inlaid lid, hand painted, made by Ceramic Art Company for O'Hara Dial Co., early 1900's, $2000-2500.

20. Beer stein, ½ liter, pottery, early 1900's, $700-1000.

**Horace Hutchinson** was best known as the author of more than a dozen popular books about golf. Twice between 1886 and 1903 he won the British Amateur Championship, and twice he was the runner-up.

**O'Hara Dial Co.** was primarily a watch dial manufacturer from 1890 to 1912 in Waltham, Massachusetts, but also manufactured the inlay lids found on steins bearing their mark. The Ceramic Art Company was commissioned to produce the bodies of the steins, complete with pewter lids into which O'Hara's inlays were inserted. These steins were marked with the O'Hara Dial Co. stamp seen here, and distributed by O'Hara Dial, so customers generally believed the company was manufacturing the stein, not just the inlay. O'Hara also distributed related items such as jugs, also made by Ceramic Art Company. The inclusion of Paris, France on the mark refers to the French location through which O'Hara Dial distributed to Europe and Japan.

21. Beer stein, ½ liter, pottery, etched, made by Hauber & Reuther, marked HR 1000 Germany, c.1900, $4000-5000.

22. Beer stein, 2 liters, 10½"h., pottery, etched, made by a Höhr-Grenzhausen factory, marked 5055, early 1900's, $6000-8000.

23. Beer stein, ½ liter, pottery, etched, made by a Höhr-Grenzhausen factory, marked 5044, early 1900's, $3000-4000.

**Höhr-Grenzhausen** is located in the Westerwald region of Germany, near Koblenz. The area has the largest concentration of ceramic manufacturers in Germany, making stoneware and pottery. Beer steins account for a large portion of the production of factories in this area.

25. Beer stein, ½ liter, pottery, incised, made by Hauber & Reuther, marked HR 1001 Germany, c.1900, $4000-5000.

24. Beer stein, ½ liter, pottery, incised, made by a Höhr-Grenzhausen factory, marked 5043, early 1900's, $3000-4000.

Hauber & Reuther was a small beer stein factory established in Freising, Germany (25 miles from Munich) in 1876. Hauber & Reuther made porcelain and stoneware steins using three part molds. They operated with a small staff of only 30 people as of 1890, primarily filling customized orders. Hauber & Reuther operated until 1910.

HR

Etching is a type of decoration typical of many German beer steins, with incised black outlining of uniformly colored design areas.

26. Beer stein, ⁴/10 liter, stoneware, made by Simon Peter Gerz, relief, saltglazed, marked 046, three golfers and a caddy, early 1900's, $3000-4000.

27. Beer stein, ½ liter, stoneware, made by Simon Peter Gerz, relief, saltglazed, marked 045, three golfers and a caddy, early 1900's, $3000-4000.

28. Beer pitcher, 2 liters, 10" h., stoneware, made by Simon Peter Gerz, relief, saltglazed, marked 040, six golfers and a caddy, early 1900's, $3500-4500.

29. Jug, 7½" h., pottery, made by Simon Peter Gerz, marked 043, four golfers and a caddy, unusual color for Gerz, early 1900's, $2000-3000.

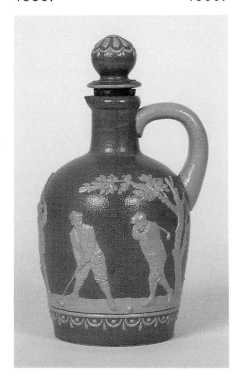

30. Jug with stopper, 9" h., stoneware, made by Simon Peter Gerz, marked 043, four golfers and a caddy, early 1900's, $3000-4000.

**Simon Peter Gerz** founded his stoneware and porcelain factory in 1857. Still in business today, the Gerz factory is presently located a few miles from Höhr-Grenzhausen, Germany.

31.    Beer stein, ½ liter, earthenware, hand painted, made by Royal Bonn, late 1800's, $6000-8000.

**Royal Bonn** was founded in 1836 by Franz Anton Mehlem for production of earthenware and porcelain in Bonn, Germany. The factory was purchased by Villeroy and Boch in 1921 and then closed 10 years later.

33.   Vase, 12" h., pottery, made by Weller Pottery - second line Dickensware, early 1900's, $1200-1800.

34.   Vase, 8½" h., pottery, made by Weller Pottery - second line Dickensware, early 1900's, $1000-1400.

35.   Vase, 8¾" h., pottery, made by Weller Pottery - second line Dickensware, early 1900's, $1000-1400.

36.   Vase, 12" h., pottery, made by Weller Pottery - second line Dickensware, early 1900's, $1200-1800.

37.   Vase, 7½" h., pottery, made by Weller Pottery - second line Dickensware, early 1900's, $1000-1400.

38.   Vase, 9¼" h., pottery, made by Weller Pottery - second line Dickensware, early 1900's, $1200-1800.

39.   Vase, 7½" h., pottery, made by Weller Pottery - second line Dickensware, early 1900's, $1000-1400.

32.   Water pitcher, 12" h., pottery, made by Weller Pottery - second line Dickensware with high glaze, early 1900's, $2000-3000.

**Weller Pottery** was named after founder Samuel A. Weller. Started in Weller's hometown of Fultonham, Ohio in 1872, the factory moved to Zanesville, Ohio in 1888, where it continued producing decorative vessels until 1949. The company was a leader in the production of various styles of art pottery. The golf motif vases produced by Weller are part of the second line of the series known as Dickensware, which were decorated with sgraffito outlines of brightly colored figures on either high glaze or light matte backgrounds.

Artists responsible for Weller Dickensware included: Anna Jewett, Anna Fulton Best, Hester Pillsbury and Hattie Mitchell. Their initials were used to mark pieces they designed.

33        34        35        36

37                38                39

40.    Pitcher, 5 ¼" h., stoneware, made by W.T. Copeland
& Sons, Ltd., early 1900's,
$1000-1400.

41.    Teapot with lid, 5" h.,
stoneware, made by W.
Copeland & Sons, Ltd., early
1900's, $1500-2000.

42.    Creamer, 4 ½" h., stone-
ware, made by W.T. Copeland
& Sons, Ltd., engraved Eva
Baring, 4th Sept. 1900 in base,
$1000-1400.

43.    Mug, 4" h., stoneware,
made by W.T. Copeland & Sons,
Ltd., early 1900's, $800-1200.

44.    Pitcher, 6" h., stoneware,
made by W.T. Copeland & Sons,
Ltd., early 1900's, $1200-
1600.

45. Milk pitcher, 7³/4" h., stoneware, made by W.T. Copeland & Sons, Ltd., early 1900's, $800-1200.

46. Jardiniere, 6³/4" h., stoneware, made by W.T. Copeland & Sons, Ltd., early 1900's, $1200-1600.

47. Three-handled cup, 5 ½" h. x 4³/4" dia., stoneware, made by W.T. Copeland & Sons, Ltd., early 1900's, $1000-1400.

**Copeland-Spode** is the modern name of a firm which dates to 1770 and follows the history of generations of Spodes and Copelands. Josiah Spode I was the master potter at the Stoke-on-Trent factory still operated by Copeland-Spode today. Josiah II opened a showroom in London where he marketed the bone china he and his father had perfected. After 1797, William Copeland managed the showroom, later succeeded by his son. Despite numerous changes of name, Copeland-Spode products have been of consistently high quality throughout the firm's history.

48.   Tankard, 8" h., stoneware with silver rim, scene in relief, made by Doulton - Lambeth, early 1900's, $1800-2400.

49.   Pitcher, 7½" h., stoneware, made by Doulton - Lambeth, decorated for Col. Bogey Whiskey, dated 1904, $2000-3000.

50.   Three handled mug, 5½" h., stoneware, made by Doulton - Lambeth, early 1900's, $1200-1600.

51.   Pitcher, 8½" h., stoneware, made by Doulton - Lambeth, early 1900's, $2000-2800.

52.   Mug, 6", stoneware with silver rim, made by Doulton - Lambeth, early 1900's, $1800-2400.

Originating as Doulton of Lambeth in 1815, **Royal Doulton** has been the name used to describe Doulton products since the Royal Warrant was granted in 1901. Doulton's stoneware vessels were made at Lambeth, designed by John Broad in art nouveau style relief. In 1877, founder John Doulton's son, Henry, acquired a Burslem pottery, where Royal Doulton figures, plates and Toby jugs are still made today. Charles Noke, Art Director at Doulton of Burslem, was the originator of Royal Doulton Series Ware, which utilized blanks in a variety of shapes and popular decorations produced using a variety of methods. Each series contained from two to more than thirty titles, or themes, and in some cases a number of different sets of characters. Different groups of characters might be found with a particular title and different titles can be found with a particular character set.

The following series included golfing scenes:

**Diversions of Uncle Toby** numbered golf as one among 15 amusements of this character from the novel *Tristam Shandy*.

**H. M. Bateman** was the designer of a satirical series of Royal Doulton scenes in the 1930's, which included:
1. The irate golfer
2. The smug golfer with club behind his back
3. The laughing caddies

**The Nineteenth Hole** was a scene of two men drinking (the title refers figuratively to the clubhouse bar.) This was a single golf scene, not part of a series.

**Proverb Series Wares** were based on the style of Will H. Bradley, a popular poster artist in the United States. Bradley drew characters for another Royal Doulton series of Eastern figures, and these were the basis for characters seen on both Proverb Series Wares and on what are known as **Golfers Series Wares**. That series includes at least 19 different views of golfers and caddies in Bradley's style, and can be found on a variety of plates, teapots and other vessels produced from 1902 until the late 1910's. Proverbs Series Wares were produced from 1911 until the late 1920's, and the proverbs which are included with golfing characters are:
1. Fine feathers make fine birds. Old saws speak the truth.
2. If at first you don't succeed try again. A miss is as good as a mile.
3. An oak is not filled by one blow. Take the will for the deed.
4. Nothing venture nothing win. Count not your chickens before thay are hatched.

**Gibson Series Wares** include a group containing predominantly golfing scenes introduced in 1904. Based on the designs of Charles Dana Gibson, the American illustrator whose Edwardian "Gibson Girl" was elevated to cult status at the turn of the century, these golfing motif titles included:
1. Golf - a good game for two.
2. Is a caddie always necessary?
3. Don't watch the player, keep your eye on the ball.
4. One difficulty of the game - keeping your eye on the ball.
5. Fore.

53          54        55          56

57.    Loving cup, 11¼" h., porcelain, made by Royal Doulton - Golf Series Ware, 1911-1932, $5000-7000.

**Golf Series Ware** was based on the style of Charles Crombie, a popular poster artist, and the illustrator of a group of prints depicting amusing aspects of the rules of golf. These were first compiled into a book by Perrier of France in 1905. The Golf series included the following five titles combined with eight different groups of characters, including golfers with or without caddies:

1. Give losers leave to speak and winners to laugh.
2. He that always complains is never pitied.
3. All fools are not knaves but all knaves are fools.
4. He hath good judgement who relieth not wholly on his own.
5. Every dog has his day and every man his hour.

These titles can be seen on a variety of plates and vessels, and were produced from 1911 to 1932.

53.    Plate, 8" x 8", porcelain, made by Royal Doulton - Golf Series Ware, inscribed *He that always complains is never pitied*, made from 1911-1932, $200-300.

54.    Jar, 5" h., porcelain, made by Royal Doulton - Golf Series Ware, 1911-1932, $400-600.

55.    Sugar shaker, 4³/₄" h. plus 1½" top, porcelain with silver top, made by Royal Doulton - Golf Series Ware, 1911-1932, $300-500.

56.    Plate, 8½" x 7¼", porcelain, made by Royal Doulton - Golf Series Ware, inscribed *Give losers leave to speak and winners to laugh*, made from 1911-1932, $250-350.

58.    Candlesticks, pair, 9" h., porcelain, made by Royal Doulton - Golf Series Ware, 1911-1932, $1200-1800.

59.    Pitcher, 11½" h., porcelain, made by Royal Doulton - Golf Series Ware, 1911-1932, $1200-1800.

60. Cup, 4" h., earthenware, made by Royal Doulton - Kingsware, 1920's, $200-300.

61. Pitcher 9" h., earthenware, made by Royal Doulton - Kingsware, 1920's, $800-1200.

62. Mug, 6" h., earthenware, made by Royal Doulton - Airbrush Brown, c.1935, $300-500.

63. Pitcher, 9½" h., earthenware, made by Royal Doulton - Airbrush Brown, c.1935, $800-1200.

64. Jug, 8¾" h., earthenware, made by Royal Doulton - Kingsware, c.1930, $800-1200.

65. Pitcher, 8½" h., stoneware with silver rim, made by Royal Doulton, Charles Crombie golf "rule" scene (see page 26), early 1900's, $1200-1600.

66.    Bud vase, 6" h., porcelain, hand painted, by Doulton - Burslem, signed J. Littler, made from 1885-1902, $6000-9000.

67.    Sugar bowl with cover, 4" h. x 4½" dia., porcelain, by Royal Doulton - Golfers Series Ware (see page 25), made from 1902-c.1918, $600-900.

**Kingsware** was the name given to a group of ceramic vessels produced by Royal Doulton using an unusual manufacturing technique. The scene was created by applying the decorative colors to the inside of the mold. These fused to the body of the vessel, formed when terra-cotta colored slip was poured into the mold and fired. The result was a soft coloration.

**Airbrush Brown** is the name given to another method of decoration used by Royal Doulton, frequently using the same subjects as Kingsware. These pieces were decorated after the ceramic body was molded and fired, and before being glazed, which provided a sharper effect with more vibrant coloring than found on Kingsware subjects. In addition, the handles, spouts and necks of this line were airbrushed brown.

68          69                    70          71

68.    Vase, 2½" h. x 4½" l. x 2¼" d., porcelain, made by Royal Doulton - Gibson Series Ware (see page 25), signed C.D. Gibson, made from 1904-c.1918, $400-600.

69.    Bud vase, 2³/4" h. x 4³/4" l. x 2" d., porcelain, made by Royal Doulton - Gibson Series Ware (see page 25), signed C.D. Gibson, made from 1904-c.1918, $400-600.

70.    Cup and saucer/dessert plate, cup is 2¼" h. x 3³/4" dia., saucer is 6¼" dia., porcelain, made by Royal Doulton - Gibson Series Ware (see page 25), signed C.D. Gibson, made from 1904-c.1918, $800-1200.

71.    Vase, 3³/4" h. x 4³/4" l. x 1½" d., porcelain, made by Royal Doulton - Gibson Series Ware (see page 25), signed C.D. Gibson, made from 1904-c.1918, $400-600.

72.    Loving cup with lid, 7½", stoneware, made by Royal Doulton - Lambeth, inscribed on front: *Molesey Hurst Golf Club*, and *Corby Challenge Cup - 1927*, $1800-2400.

73.    Plate, 10³/8" d., porcelain, made by Royal Doulton - Proverb Series Ware (see page 25), inscribed *Fine feathers make fine birds. Old Saws speak the truth*, made from 1911-c.1928, $150-250.

74.    Plate, 10¼" d., porcelain, made by Royal Doulton - Golfers Series Ware (see page 25), unusual border, made from 1911-c.1928, $200-300.

75.    Pitcher, 15" h., with 2 mugs, ½ liter, porcelain, unmarked, c.1920, pitcher, $4000-6000, mugs, $600-900 each.

76.    Plate, 7½" d., porcelain, made by Grimwades, Stoke on Trent, caption reads *The Brownies(Golf)*, legend on back reads *Brownies are little imaginary sprites, who delight in harmless pranks and helpful deeds they work and sport while weary households sleep and never are seen by mortal eyes*, c.1910, $200-300.

77.    Plate, 10½" d., porcelain, made by Royal Doulton - Golf Series Ware (see page 26), made from 1911-1932, $200-300.

78.    Plate, 7½" d., porcelain, made by Taylor, Smith & Taylor Company - Latona line, c.1910, depicts Brownies, $75-125.

79.    Cereal bowl, 6" d., porcelain, by Royal Doulton - Bunnykins, 1930's, $200-300.

80.    Plate, 7½" d., pottery, made by Royal Doulton - Bunnykins, 1930's, $100-200.

81. Plaque, 10" d., porcelain, early 1900's, $1800-2400.

82. Plaque, 11" d., pottery, designed by Viktor Schreckengost, Art Deco, early 1930's, $1500-2000.

**Taylor, Smith & Taylor Company** produced porcelain and semi-porcelain dinner and toilet sets in Chester, West Virginia beginning in 1899. In 1973, the firm was purchased and became the Ceramic Division of Anchor Hocking Glass Company, and closed in 1982.

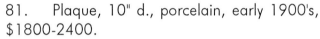

**Viktor Schreckengost** was an American sculptor and ceramic designer, who worked at various times for several American ceramics firms as well as independently. He was the recipient of several awards for his contributions to the field of ceramics. Plaque #82 may be found with or without the Cowan factory mark.

**Bunnykins** were designed by Barbara Vernon Bailey, the daughter of Doulton - Burslem's general manager Cuthbert Bailey. First produced in 1934, Bunnykins soon supplanted all of Royal Doulton's other children's patterns. After WWII, her designs inspired the work of Walter Hayward, some of whose designs are still in production.

The **Brownies** were a group of cartoon characters popularized during the 1890's.

83.    Figure, 14" h., pottery, made by Amphora Pottery Works, marked Amphora Work, Reissner, c.1910, $1500-2000.

84.    Figure, 11" h., porcelain, marked Germany, 1930's, $400-600.

**Amphora  Pottery Works** was a manufacturer of stoneware and porcelain in Turn-Teplitz, Bohemia (now Czechoslovakia). Founded in 1892 by Hans Riessner, Carl Riessner, Eduard Stellmacher and Rudolf Kessel, the firm adopted the title Amphora in 1903. The mark may include the word Austria, since Bohemia was part of the empire of Austria-Hungary before WWII.

85.    Match holder, 3¹/8", porcelain, made by MacIntyre, early 1900's, $500-700.

86.    Humidor with lock top, 5¼" h., porcelain, made by Wiltshaw & Robinson, made from 1899 to the 1920's, $700-1000.

87.    Match bowl, 2³/4" h., porcelain, made by Wiltshaw & Robinson, made from 1899 to the 1920's, $250-350.

**MacIntyre** was an English manufacturer of porcelain and earthenware, located in Burslem, Staffordshire, England from around 1860 to 1928.

**Wiltshaw & Robinson** operated the Carlton Works in Stoke-on-Trent, Staffordshire, England beginning in 1890; since 1957, the firm has been called **Carlton Ware Ltd**. Wiltshaw & Robinson produced ornamental porcelain and earthenware items, including vases, teapots and water jugs.

88.    Biscuit jar, 5¼" h., porcelain with silver rim and lid, made by MacIntyre, rim and lid both have hallmark: Birmingham 1897, $1500-2000.

89.    Humidor, 4½" h., stone-ware, marked A Rogers Product, Made in England, 1920's, $600-900.

90.    Humidor, 5¼" h., pottery, made by Taylor-Tunnecliffe, c.1885-1898, $1200-1600.

91.    Humidor, 5¼" h., pottery, marked A.F.C. Patent, special top with expansion closure for tight fit, 1920's, $800-1200.

92.    Humidor, 7½" h., porcelain, made by A.G. Richardson & Co., Ltd., cartoon type decoration, dated 1925, $600-900.

93.    Humidor, 6½" h., porcelain, inscribed *Coupe Vittellirse*, cartoon type decoration, 1920's, $600-900.

**Taylor-Tunnecliffe** was a manufacturer of earthenware and porcelain wares in Hanley, Staffordshire, England around 1875 to 1898.

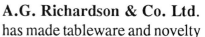

**A.G. Richardson & Co. Ltd.** has made tableware and novelty items under the trade name Crown Ducal, in Tunstall, Staffordshire, England, since 1915.

94. Toothpick holder, 1½" h., porcelain, made by The Foley China Co. (see page 39), c.1920, $150-250.

95. Match holder, 1½" h., pottery, late 1800's, $300-400.

96. Match holder, 1½" h., pottery with a silver rim, late 1800's, $300-400.

97. Tooth pick holder, 2½" h., porcelain, made by Royal Doulton - Golf Series Ware (see page 26), 1911-1932, $300-400.

98. Pipe, 5" l., porcelain bowl, made by Royal Copenhagen, c.1950, $250-350.

99. Perfume bottle, 2½" h., pottery, marked S & S, late 1890's, $75-125.

**Royal Copenhagen Porcelain Factory** was a Danish firm operating privately when it first began operation as the Danish Porcelain Factory in 1775. It was supported by the Danish Royal family from 1775 until 1867, when it was purchased by A. Falch, a private owner. The firm changed hands again in 1882 and was moved to Smalzgade, where it is still operating.

100. Cup and saucer, cup is 2¼" h., saucer 5" d., porcelain, made by Taylor & Smith & Taylor (see page 33), depicts Brownies, c.1910, $300-400.

101. Ash tray, 5½" w., porcelain, signed Brown, c.1920, $150-250.

102. Ash tray, 6½" w., porcelain, made by A.G. Richardson & Co., Ltd. (see page 36), c.1930, $200-300.

103. Pitcher, 4" h., porcelain, made by The Foley China Co., 1920's, $300-400.

104. Dish, 7" x 6", porcelain, made by The Foley China Co., 1920's, $200-300.

105. Cup and saucer, cup is 2½" h., saucer is 5" d., porcelain, made by Wiltshaw & Robinson (see page 35), marked Carlton Ware, made from 1899 to the 1920's, $250-350.

**Nippon**, the Japanese name for Japan, was used to mark Japanese exports to satisfy the United States' import laws. Much of the porcelain exported from Japan was manufactured by the Noritake Company (see page 42).

106      107              108          109              110

106.   Bread plate, 5¼" d., porcelain, made by The Foley China Co., marked Foley Art China, England, Peacock Pottery, inscribed *Scotscraig Golf House* and *flag staff and club with Scotscraig Bazaar October, 1906*, $100-200.

107.   Demitasse cup & saucer, cup is 2¼" h., saucer is 4⅝" dia., porcelain, made by The Foley China Co., marked Foley Art China, England, Peacock Pottery, inscribed *Scotscraig Golf House* and *flag staff and club with Scottscraig Bazaar October, 1906*, $100-200.

108.   Salad plate, 8½" d., porcelain, made by New York & Rudolstadt Pottery, marked Schwarzburg, signed Landry, c.1915, $400-600.

109.   Ashtray, 4¼" d., porcelain, marked Hand Painted Nippon, c.1920, $100-200.

110.   Mug, 4" h., porcelain, unmarked, cartoon style decoration, 1930's, $250-350.

**Foley Potteries** was founded in the 1820's by John Smith in Fenton, Staffordshire, England. The firm was later controlled by Henry Wileman and then his sons, and thereafter by the Shelley family, who replaced the Foley trade name with their own. It was while the firm was still operating as **Wileman & Co.**, prior to 1925, that the golf collectibles shown in this chapter were produced.

**Schwarzburg** is the trade name for New York & Rudolstadt Pottery, porcelain manufacturers from 1882 to 1932 in Rudolstadt, Germany.

111          112          113

114          115          116

117. Cigarette holder, match holder & striker, 5" h., pottery, dated 1930, $200-300.

118. Tooth pick holder, 5" h., earthenware, 1930's, $200-300.

119. Cigarette holder, 5" h., porcelain, marked E-9286, c.1940, $50-100.

120. Figure, 6" h., bisque-glazed porcelain, marked Germany, c.1930, $200-300.

111. Figural bottle, 9" h., porcelain, marked Germany, 1950's, $300-450.

112. Ashtray with figure, 5" h. figure, porcelain, marked with crown & slashed "S", c.1930, $100-200.

113. Match holder & striker, 9½" h. figure, pottery, 1890's, $600-900.

114. Vase, 6½" h., pottery, majolica, marked Austria, c.1910, $300-450.

115. Pin tray, 3½" h., porcelain, marked 7970, 1930's, $75-125.

116. Tobacco jar, 7" h., porcelain, marked Germany, c.1930, $400-600.

121. Figure, 3" h., porcelain, made by Crown Staffordshire China Company, 1906-1930, $20-40.

122. Toothpick holder, 3½" h., porcelain, marked Made in Germany, 1930's, $100-200.

123. Figure, 3½" h., porcelain, marked Patent Applied for No. 9034-7 Made in Japan, 1930's, $100-200.

124. Condiment set, 4" h., porcelain, made by S. Fielding and Co., Ltd., 1913-1930, $100-200.

125. Cup and saucer, cup is 3" h., saucer is 6½" d., porcelain, made by Royal Worcester, modern, retail around $60.

**Crown Devon** is the trade name for the products of **S. Fielding and Co., Ltd.** The Stoke-on-Trent, Staffordshire, England pottery, has produced earthenware and porcelain domestic wares since 1870.

Since 1948, **Crown Staffordshire China Co. Ltd.** has been the name of the porcelain manufacturer founded in 1847 by Thomas Green as the Minerva Works in Fenton, Staffordshire, England.

**Noritake** was a Japanese porcelain factory which opened in 1904 in Nagoya, Japan; its production consisted primarily of western motifs on tableware meant for export. Noritake was the manufacturer which produced much of the group of wares marked Nippon, Japanese for the country of origin required to be marked on imports to the United States after 1894.

**Rookwood Pottery** was founded in Cincinnati, Ohio in 1880 by Maria Longworth Nichols Storer. By the early 1900's, individually decorated and signed wares were supplemented by unsigned mass-produced products. After a series of financial difficulties and ownership changes, the pottery finally closed in 1967.

126. Mug, 3½" h., porcelain, c.1910, $75-125.

127. Cup, 4" h., porcelain, made by Wileman & Co. (see The Foley Potteries on page 39), dated 1901, $300-400.

128. Beer mug, ½ liter, pottery, made by Royal Doulton (see page 25), signed H.M. Bateman, c.1937, $600-900.

129. Beer mug, ½ liter, porcelain, marked Nippon, (see page 38), 1930's, $600-800.

130. Humidor, 5½" h., porcelain, marked Aonian, probably 1920's, $500-700.

131. Cigarette holder and ash tray, 9½" h., pottery, made by Rookwood Pottery, c.1950, $200-300.

132. Humidor, 6½" h., porcelain, made by Noritake, 1930's, $500-700.

133. Plate, 10¼" d., porcelain, made by Warwick China Company, signed by Victor Venner, titled *One up and one to play*, 1920's, $200-300.

134. Plate, 10½" d., porcelain, inscribed *Carry your Caddie, Sir?*, 1920's, $200-300.

135. Plate, 9 ³/8" d., porcelain, inscribed *The Indispensable Caddie*, 1920's, $200-300.

136. Plate, 9" d., porcelain, inscribed *Golf Critics*, 1920's, $200-300.

137. Plate, 9" d., porcelain, made by Warwick China Company, Bobby Jones pictured, c.1930, $150-250.

138. Plate, 9" d., porcelain, made by Warwick China Company, *Culbertsen Hills* on front, dated 1931, $100-200.

139. Beer mug, ½ liter, porcelain, made by Rosenthal, signed Edna Albright, old Scotch caddy, c.1920, $600-900.

140. Beer mug, ½ liter, stoneware, made by Robinson Clay Products Co., c.1915, $300-500.

141. Pitcher, 5" h., porcelain, made by Royal Doulton - Uncle Toby Series Ware (see page 25), made from 1909-1930, $400-600.

**Robinson Clay Products Company** was the name adopted in 1902, for a pottery manufacturing firm begun in 1856 in Akron, Ohio. After joining with Ransbottom Brothers in 1920, Robinson Clay Products Company became the wholesale facility for the firm, and established outlets throughout the East coast and even outside the country.

142. Tile, 6" x 6", earthenware, marked No.6, 1800's, $250-350.

**Warwick China Company** produced porcelain domestic and hotel dinner wares in Wheeling, West Virginia beginning in 1884. The firm incorporated in 1887 and continued production until 1951.

**Rosenthal** was founded by Philip Rosenthal in 1879 in Selb, Bavaria (now Germany), producing high quality figures and tableware; he revived the firm following extensive damage during WWII and it continues to operate today.

143.    Beer mug, ½ liter, pottery, made by Dartmouth Pottery Ltd., after 1947, $75-125.

144.    Beer mug, ½ liter, pottery, made by Dartmouth Pottery, Ltd., after 1947, $75-125.

145.    Beer mug, ½ liter, stoneware, similar to #140, but maker is unknown, c.1915, $100-200.

146.    Beer mug, ½ liter, pottery, made by Burgess & Leigh, marked Burleigh Ironstone Staffordshire England, Art Deco style, modern, $100-200.

147.    Beer mug, ½ liter, pottery, made by Royal Bradwell, marked Arthur Wood England Sports Series, modern, $50-100.

148.    Pitcher, 7" h., stoneware, made by W.T. Copeland & Sons, Ltd. (see page 23), c.1920, $500-700.

**Burgess & Leigh** began production of ceramics in 1862, and is still in business in Staffordshire, England.

*Burleigh*

STAFFORDSHIRE
ENGLAND

**Dartmouth   Pottery, Ltd.** began production of ceramics in 1947 in Dartmouth, Devon, England.

149. Figurine, *Waiting to Tee Off,* 11½" h., porcelain, made by Lladro, first issued in 1985 at $145, retail price around $240.

150. Figurine, *Golfer,* 12" h., porcelain, made by Lladro, issued in 1973 at $66, retail price around $260.

151. Figurine, *Golfer,* 10" h., porcelain, made by Royal Doulton, marked HN 2992, dated 1988, retail price around $175.

**Lladro** is a manufacturer of porcelain figurines opened in 1951 by Juan, Jose and Vicente Lladro in Valencia, Spain. The Lladro Collectors Society is an excellent source of information about Lladro collectibles, and can be reached at P.O. Box 1122, 43 West 57th Street, New York, NY 10101.

LLADRÓ

152.   Pilsner beer goblet, ½ liter, stoneware, relief, tournament trophy cup in rear, made by A.J. Thewalt, modern, retail around $30.

153.   Beer stein, ¾ liter, stoneware, relief, other color combination versions exist, made by A.J. Thewalt, limited edition of 10,000, retail around $200.

154.   Beer stein, ½ liter, stoneware, transfer decoration, two golfing scenes, made in Germany, modern, retail around $35.

A.J. Thewalt has been a stoneware manufacturer in Höhr-Grenzhausen, Germany since 1893.

mark since 1930

155.   Character jug, 7" h., pottery, made by Royal Doulton, marked Golfer D6623 Copr. 1970, first produced in 1971, retail around $80.

# GLASS

As with ceramics, most glass golf art was produced in England or the United States, and the majority of glass items served a purpose related to drinking or smoking.

## MATERIALS

Glass is produced from a combination of refined sand, an alkali (either potash or soda) to lower the melting temperature of the sand, and in the finest glass, the relatively expensive ingredient, lead. Mineral oxides are used, just as they are in ceramic materials, to impart color to the glass. Varying the quantities and combinations of those minerals provides a multitude of color possibilities. For instance, large quantities of manganese and iron oxide are required to produce the clear black color of items #161 to 163. Lesser quantities of manganese silicate, however, are responsible for the amethyst purple of biscuit jar #184. To obtain colorless glass, manganese must be used in still smaller quantity to neutralize the presence of iron in the sand, which would otherwise impart a green or amber tinge to the glass mixture.

## DECORATION

Most golf motif glass was decorated by one or more of the following methods. Many glass items are decorated by techniques which impart a texture or design to the glass surface, including etching, engraving or cutting. Alone or in combination with these methods, a second color can be added by overlay, flashing or staining. Finally, enameling can be used to create a many-colored design on the surface of the glass.

Etching involves coating the glass with wax, through which the desired pattern is drawn. The wax prevents the acid that is then applied from acting on any but the design areas. Water is applied to stop the action of the acid.

Engraving requires a sharp instrument, usually a copper wheel, to physically remove pieces of glass to create the design. Copper-wheel engraving is a very detailed and precise art, using wheels of up to 150 different sizes, some as small as a pin head to achieve the desired result.

When techniques such as overlay, flashing or staining are employed to add a second color on top of the base color, the outermost layer is either mechanically engraved or chemically etched to show through to the color underneath. Overlaid glass is produced by touching the blob of molten glass of the base color to a blob of another color, of which it picks up a thin outer layer. Flashed glass has a thin layer of colored translucent enamel fired onto its surface. Finally, a second color could be added by staining the surface with metallic oxides, the same ones which could be used to color the body of the glass when combined in the glass mixture, as explained above. This stained glass is sometimes cut through to reveal the base color.

Cut glass describes a design which is essentially three-dimensional. It is achieved by first making the deepest cuts of the design into a blank (the undecorated bare glass to be cut), using steel wheels with mitered edges onto which wet sand would drip to aid in the process. Next comes the refinement of the design using hard stone wheels and the action of dripping water to aid the "smoothing", as this step was known. Finally, the object could be polished, first on a wooden wheel, then on a buffing wheel.

Several methods of lowering the costs of the cutting process were introduced at various points in the history of cutting. In the early 1890's, acid-polishing was introduced as a shortcut to finishing cut glass. Detractors found fault with the results of acid polishing when used to avoid polishing and buffing, but it was one way in which costs could be reduced in the United States to compete with the vastly lower wage scales of the European glass manufacturers. Around 1900, the use of pressed blanks into which the basic pattern was pressed, and had only to be refined, began to replace the initial "roughing" stage of cutting glass. Pressed blanks were made using a mold into which the glass was forced by a plunger. The use of pressed blanks was an obvious cost-cutting efficiency, but markedly lowered the quality of the final product.

Glass golf art was often enameled, sometimes in addition to one of the above methods. The enamel was made from glass with coloring derived from various mineral oxides.

Glass was also frequently decorated with silver accents, some with silver rims and other edging, while others were partially or entirely overlaid with silver. The overlay usually fits tightly around the finished glass shape, and is attached to the glass with an adhesive.

156.   Bottle, 10" h., sterling silver on glass, c.1920, $400-600.

157.   Bottle, 11½" h., sterling silver on glass, c.1920, $500-700.

## COLLECTING

There exists a risk that glass golf art could be reproduced, particularly that engraved decorations might be duplicated. Nonetheless, to date this has not happened to the best of our knowledge. There are, however, some new items being produced, which can clearly be distinguished from old items by their design, especially by the style of apparel worn by the subjects.

As with all areas of glass collecting, clear glass predominates in availability; therefore, colored pieces are usually harder to find and command higher prices as a result.

158.   Cocktail set, shaker 11" h., six tumblers (two pictured) 5½" h., six goblets (two pictured) 3 ³/4" h., sterling silver on glass, c.1920, $1800-2600.

159.   Bottle, 7" h., sterling silver on glass, c.1920, $600-800.

160.   Glass, 3 ¼" h., frosted glass with silver overlay, dated 1920, $100-200.

161                                    162                                    163

164.  Tantalus, 9 ½" h., sterling silver on glass, silver plated holder & cups, Art Deco, c.1920, $500-700.

165.  Wine bottle, 11" h., sterling silver on glass, c.1920, $400-600.

161.  Scotch decanter, 9" h., sterling silver on glass, c.1920, $600-800.

162.  Decanter, 10½" h., sterling silver on glass, c.1920, $400-600.

163.  Flask, 5³/4" h., sterling silver on glass, c.1920, $400-600.

Note: Overlays are usually marked **STERLING**

166.   Pitcher with insert for ice, 13" h., sterling silver on glass with chrome plated top, three different figures shown, c.1920, $600-900.

167.   Wine bottle, 14½" h., sterling silver on glass, unusual green color, c.1920, $600-900.

168.   Cocktail pitcher, 17" h., sterling silver on glass, c.1920, $600-900.

169.   Smoking set, ashtray 3½" x 5", box 3¼" x 4¼" x 2¼" deep, intaglio cut, late 1920's, $300-400.

170.   Cigarette box, 3½" x 4½" x 1½" deep, intaglio cut, late 1920's, $200-300.

172. Ash tray, 2½" x 2½", acid etched glass, c.1940, $50-100.

174

175

176

171. Ash tray, 5" x 3", intaglio cut, made by Hoffman, c.1925, $400-600.

173. Ash tray, 4" x 3", acid etched glass, c.1940, $100-200.

**Heinrich Hoffman** was a Czechoslovakian who started a firm in Paris before 1900, and around 1900, founded another company in Bohemia. Around the mid-1920's, Hoffman developed a technique to produce pressed and frosted glass, with the appearance of a cut design. The process is known as "intaglio cutting".

174. Cigarette box, 3" x 5" x 2" deep, sterling silver on glass, c.1920, $300-400.

175. Ash tray, 6" d., sterling silver on glass, matches cigarette box below, c.1940, $150-250.

176. Cigarette box, 5½" x 4" x 1½" deep, sterling silver on glass, matches ash tray above, c.1940, $200-300.

**T. G. Hawkes & Co.** was founded in 1880 in Corning, New York by Thomas Hawkes. He had worked at Hoare & Dailey for 10 years, and obviously left on amicable terms, since he was able to purchase glass blanks from a firm which had previously sold only to Hoare & Dailey. Hawkes was famous for both cut and engraved glass. He won the Grand Prize at the Universal Exposition in Paris in 1889. Hawkes financed the establishment of the Steuben Glass Works in 1903, seemingly to ensure his supply of glass blanks. In 1912, Hawkes opened a department to make silver mounts which had previously been purchased from Gorham and other vendors. The firm continued to prosper through the 1930's despite occasional difficulties, but the business declined beginning in the 1940's and was finally liquidated in 1962.

177. Martini pitcher & strainer, 17" h., engraved glass, made by T.G. Hawkes & Co., c.1920, $600-900.

178. Decanter, 13" h., engraved glass, Art Deco, 1930's, $250-350.

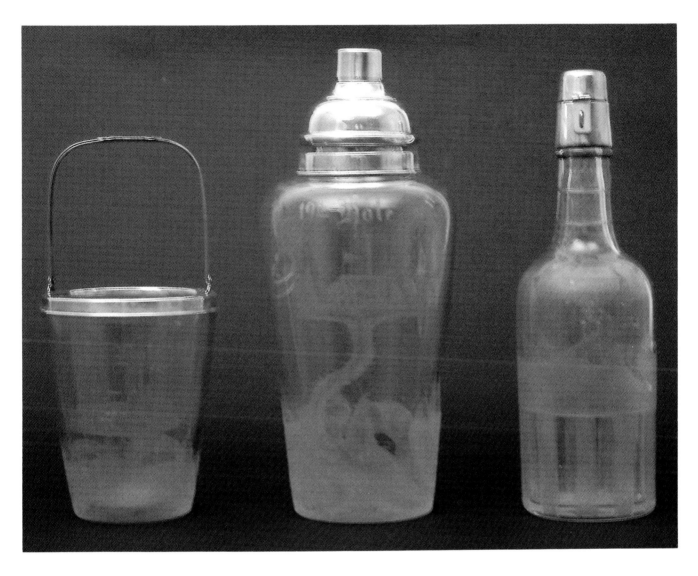

179. Ice bucket, 6" h., engraved glass with sterling silver rim & handle, made by T.G. Hawkes & Co., c.1900, $300-500.

180. Cocktail shaker, 13" h., engraved glass with silver plated top, made by T.G. Hawkes & Co., c.1900, $600-900.

181. Wine bottle, 12" h., engraved glass with silver cap, made by T.G. Hawkes & Co., c.1900, $300-500.

182.    Glasses & tray, tray 7" h. x 7" l. x 7" d., glasses 4½" h., etched, made by Cambridge Glass Company, 1920's, $400-600.

183.    Goblet, 3¾" h., etched, made by Cambridge Glass Company, 1920's, $50-100.

184.    Humidor with top, 5½" h., etched scene in gold, made by Cambridge Glass Company, top has moisturizer section attached, 1920's, $400-600.

**Cambridge Glass Company** was incorporated in 1901 in Cambridge, Ohio. Golf motif glass wares were available by the 1920's. Collectors may wish to contact: National Cambridge Collectors, Inc. at P.O. Box 416, Cambridge, Ohio 43725.

**C. F. Monroe Company** began in 1880 in Meriden, Connecticut and was incorporated in 1892. The firm's most popular product was an opal white glass, of which there were three lines, including Wave Crest Ware.

185.    Ashtray, 1⅝" h. x 4¼" d., gold plated rim, golf ball and club, made by The C.F. Monroe Company, marked Wavecrest, 1901, $400-600.

186. Decanter, 10"h., cut glass, possibly made by Mt. Washington Glass Company (The Pairpoint Corporation), 1920's, $600-900.

187. Decanter, 12" h., .999 silver on glass, the silver was made by Black, Starr & Frost, inscribed *Shinnecock Hills Golf Club*, c.1916, $1000-1400.

**Mt. Washington Glass Works** was founded in 1837 in Boston, Massachusetts, but moved to New Bedford, Massachusetts in 1870. After reorganizing in 1876, the Mt. Washington Glass Company merged with Pairpoint Manufacturing Co. in 1894 to become the Pairpoint Corporation, which operated until 1929.

**Black, Starr & Frost** of New York traces its roots to Savannah, Georgia in the early 1800's. It has long been a retailer as well as a manufacturer of products under its own name, and though the firm is no longer a manufacturer, some of the products it sells carry its trademark.

188. Vase, 15" h., milk glass and metal, transfer decoration, made by The Handel Company, c.1910, $1000-1500.

189. Humidor, 3¼" h. x 5¼" w., milk glass with copper lid, transfer decoration, made by The Handel Company, c.1910, $800-1200.

190. Vase, 11¾" h., green, enameled, possibly Loetz, c.1900, $6000-9000.

**Loetz** is an Austrian manufacturer of glass, known for wares colored with lustre or irridescent finishes produced in large quantities in the early 1900's.

191. Pitcher & tumblers, pitcher 11" h., tumblers 5½" h., probably German, c.1910, $1800-2400.

**The Handel Company** was founded as a partnership between Adolph Eyden and Philip Julius Handel in 1885. Located in Meriden, Connecticut, the firm became Handel's alone in 1893, and was incorporated in 1903; it continued operations until 1936.

192. Bottle, 8" h., hand painted, c.1930, $300-400.

193. After shave bottle, Fore!, 9½" h., made by AR Winarick Co., Art Deco, dated 1920, $150-250.

194. Glass, 6½" h., hand painted, c.1930, $75-125.

195. Set of four glasses, 3" h., different golfer on each, c.1930, $100-200 for the set.

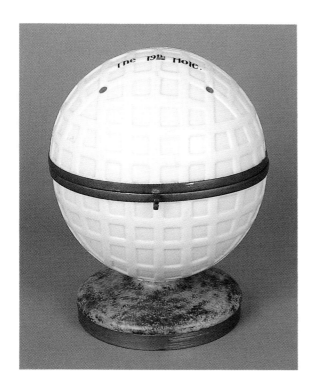

196.   Cordial set, contains bottle & set of glasses, 9" h. x 7" d., inscribed *The 19th Hole*, marked Czechoslovakia, c.1940, $300-500.

197.   Perfume bottle, 8" h., cut glass, marked Czechoslovakia, Art Deco, c.1930, $600-900.

198.   Tumbler, 5" h., glass with sterling overlay, made by De Passe Mfg. Co., c.1914, $100-200.

199.   Paperweight, 4½" h., marked Tiffany & Co., c.1970, $50-100.

**De Passe Manufacturing Company** of New York manufactured silver and gold mounted glass around 1910. The company was succeeded by Depasse, Pearsall Silver Co.

# SILVER & GOLD

 Sterling silver and silver plated golf art objects were very popular even before the turn of the twentieth century, both as trophies and as decorative accessories. Silver was frequently used for general decorative purposes because it is easy to work with and readily available, while being much less expensive than gold. Gold was quite popular in production of small accessories, such as brooches or medals.

## MATERIAL

Sterling silver is an alloy of at least 925 parts pure silver and 75 parts of another metal, usually copper. This proportion provides the best combination of strength, malleability and beauty, with minimal wear to the designs made with it. Other grades of silver typically range from 800 to 900 parts silver.

Silver plating was an ancient craft, revived in the 1740's to provide a low cost substitute for sterling silver. The modern electroplating method was patented in 1840. A base metal, such as copper, was immersed in a solution through which an electric current was passed, causing silver to be deposited on the object. Depending on the quality and thickness of the plating, in time it might be worn through to the base metal. When wear or damage to the plating occurs, the item can be replated and usually made to look just like the original, if repaired by an expert. However, the cost of doing so may be excessive relative to the increased value of the item being repaired. Silver plated items are generally less expensive than similar sterling silver objects.

Sterling silver may be identified in several ways. American and European sterling silver is sometimes marked with the word STERLING or by the number 925, the number of thousandth parts of pure silver. English manufacturers use a hallmark to designate the silver content. The hallmark consists of three elements: the mark of origin, showing the city where the piece was assayed, the date letter, showing the year of manufacture, and the assay mark, a lion "passant", verifying the content to be sterling. [See the Bibliography for books which list hallmarks.]

Silver plated wares have various marks as well, though at times no marks at all are present to indicate that the items is in fact plated. Marks used on silver plated wares include: EPNS for Electro Plated Nickel Silver, EPBM for Electro Plated Base Metal, and EPC for Electro Plated Copper.

Gold items can be made with pure, 24 karat gold, or alloyed with copper. Karat weights are a measure of the number of twenty-fourth parts of gold content. Thus, 18 karat gold is 75% gold and 25% copper. The lowest karat weight typically found is 9 karat gold.

## COLLECTING

The majority of silver golf art was made in England and the United States, from about 1890 to 1940. Unger Bros., a well known American silversmith, had a stock catalog in 1902 showing many items with the figure of a golfer or a caddie. Tiffany & Co., The Gorham Mfg. Company, Wm. B. Kerr & Co. and Frank M. Whiting Co., as well as a host of smaller silversmiths also produced golf motifs to fill the demand for trophies and gifts for golfers. Still other companies made souvenir spoons with golf scenes.

Recently, several nineteenth century pieces of English silver have been seen, to which enameled golf scenes have been added, in an effort to "produce" a golf motif antique. Collectors should know the source and check the reliability of any enameled sterling.

The reproduction of sterling or silver plated pieces themselves is much more difficult than enameling. There have been instances in which castings of antique flatware have been produced, but the quality has been obviously lacking. Examples of golf motif silver reproductions are showing up in stores and at antique markets. While some are easily identified because of modern dress styles, some old designs are being copied, and a collector should pay close attention to date marks.

200.   Jewel box, 8½" l. x 5½" d. x 2½" h., sterling, c.1905, $3000-4000.

201.   Wine cooler, 8½" h., sterling, enameled, made by Gorham, c.1898, expensive.

**The Gorham Corporation** was founded by Jabez Gorham with four partners around 1816 in Providence, Rhode Island. The name of the firm changed several times before 1865, when it was incorporated as The Gorham Mfg. Company. In 1868, the firm adopted sterling silver (925/1000 parts silver) as their standard, and began to use the tradmark shown below on all silver pieces. Gorham acquired numerous other silver manufacturers over the years. Gorham was purchased by Textron, Inc. in 1967.

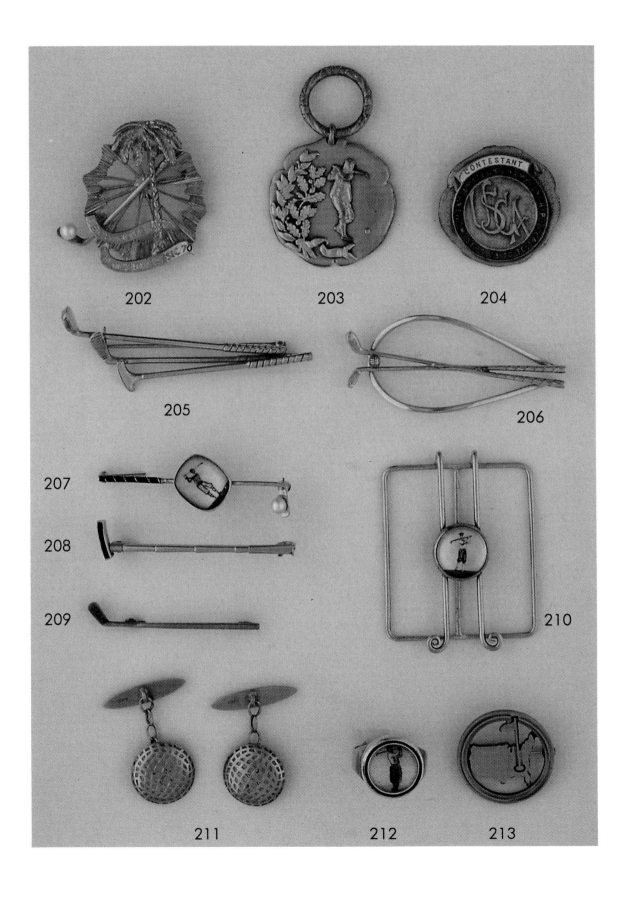

202            203            204

205                           206

207

208                                          210

209

211            212            213

202. Brooch, 1½" x 1½", 14 karat gold with pearl ball, *Bob Hope Desert Classic*, probably a gift to participants' wives, 1970, $400-600.

203. Medal, 1¼" x 1¼", gold, *Upper Montclair Country Club Golf Championship 1910*, $300-500.

204. Pin, 1¼" d., gold plated, enameled, for contestants in the Women's Amateur Championship September 25 to 30, 1922, $75-125.

205. Lapel pin, 2½", 14 karat gold, three clubs, c.1950's, $300-500.

206. Money clip, 2½", 14 karat gold, 1930's - 1940's, $300-500.

207. Lapel pin, 2", 14 karat gold with pearl ball, reverse painting on glass with black enameled grip, c.1920's, $300-400.

208. Lapel pin, 2", platinum grip, gold and sapphire putter head, 1930's or later, $300-400.

209. Lapel pin, 1¾", gold and silver, dated 1935, $100-200.

210. Money clip, 1⅛" x 2", 14 karat gold, reverse painting on glass, 1920's, $300-500.

211. Cuff links, ¾" d., 9.375 karat gold, 1920's, $150-250.

212. Man's ring, ⅝" d., silver and enamel, 1920's, $150-250.

213. Lapel pin, 1", marked ¹/₁₀ 10 karat gold filled, Augusta National Golf Club insignia, 1960's, $30-60.

214. Watch fob, 8¼" l. with chain, sterling, enameled, c.1920, $75-125.

215. Lady's pin, 2" x 2½", sterling, made by Fishel, Nessler & Co. N.Y., c.1910, $300-500.

216. Medal, 2" d., sterling, hallmark: J.A.R., Birmingham, 1920, $300-500.

217. Chatelaine, 4" l. with chain, sterling, c.1910, $250-350.

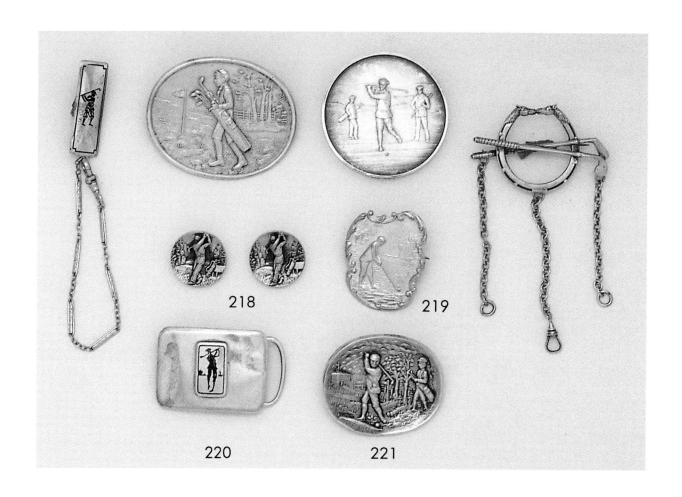

218. Cuff links or men's blazer buttons, 1" d., sterling, 1930's, $200-300.

219. Lady's pin, 1¼" x 1½", sterling, made by F.S. Gilbert, c.1910, $300-400.

220. Belt buckle, 1¼" x 1³/4", sterling, enameled, made by James E. Blake Company, c.1910, $300-400.

221. Lady's pin, 2" d., sterling, c.1910, $300-400.

**Fishel, Nessler** manufactured sterling and other types of jewelry in New York, from the 1890's until the late 1930's.

**F.S. Gilbert** manufactured sterling silver articles in North Attleboro, Massachusetts in the early 1900's.

**STERLING**

**James E. Blake Company** was founded in 1898 in Attleboro, Massachusetts by James Blake, William Blake and Lefferts Hoffman. In 1905, the firm received a patent for production of sterling and 14 karat gold inlaid silver smoking accessories, pocket knives and belt buckles.

222. Medal, 1¼" x 2", 14 karat gold, made by Tiffany & Co., dated 1926, $1200-1800.

223. Medal, 1¼" x 1³/4", 14 karat gold, inscribed *Ridgemoor Country Club*, dated 1920, $400-600.

**Tiffany & Co.** was founded in 1837 as a retailer of fine goods in New York under the name Tiffany & Young, which became Tiffany, Young & Ellis in 1841. At that time, Young went to Europe and initiated what would remain close ties to European suppliers. The visit eventually led to opening stores in Paris and London.

In 1845, silver formed only a small part of Tiffany's offerings, according to a catalog of their wares. Their business was predominantly stationery, porcelain, glass, bronzes, and miscellany ranging from papier mâché to moccasins. Around 1848, Tiffany began to manufacture silver flatware and holloware, under the design direction of Gustav Herter. In 1951, Herter left Tiffany & Co., and perhaps not coincidentally, Tiffany arranged for the exclusive production of holloware by John C. Moore. After his retirement, his son Edward C. Moore took over and led Tiffany to preeminence in the production of silver, especially in detail-intensive, custom designed wares. The arrangement with Moore was exclusive only in one direction, as Tiffany continued to purchase silver articles from other manufacturers. The fame earned by Tiffany where silver products were concerned can be largely attributed to Edward Moore.

In 1853, Tiffany & Co. emerged as the name of the firm following founder Charles Lewis Tiffany's buyout of his two partners. Tiffany & Co. continues to operate today.

Marks on Tiffany products seen in this chapter read **TIFFANY & CO. MAKERS** and either the words **STERLING** or **14K GOLD**, depending upon the material, in addition to the initial of the president of the company at the time the piece was produced.

**Unger Bros.** was organized in 1872 in Newark, New Jersey to manufacture pocket knives and other hardware; in a few years they began producing silver jewelry. The wife of Eugene Unger, Emma Dickinson, was the designer of the Art Nouveau style design characteristic of Unger Bros, and much imitated by other manufacturers. By 1910, these patterns had been abandoned in favor of simpler forms, and in 1919, Unger Bros. was sold.

224.   Match safe, 2" x 2¼", sterling, made by Unger Bros., c.1900, $600-900.

225.   Match safe, 2" x 2¼", sterling, Art Nouveau, c.1900, $500-700.

226.   Match safe, 1½" x 2¾", sterling, c.1890, $500-700.

227.   Match safe, 1½" x 2 ½", sterling, marked with an arrow and "S", c.1910, $400-600.

228.   Match safe, 1½" x 2½", sterling, made by Gorham (see page 65), c.1910, $400-600.

229.   Match safe, 1¼" x 2 ¼", sterling, c.1890, $350-500.

230.   Match safe, 1 ¹/10" x 1³/4", sterling, made by La Pierre Mfg. Co., c.1900, $200-300.

231.   Match safe, shape of a golf ball, 1³/4" d., sterling, hallmark: H.W. Ld., Birmingham, 1905, $500-700.

232.   Match safe, 1³/8" x 2", sterling, c.1900, $300-400.

**La Pierre Mfg. Co.** began in 1888 as a New York shop where Frank H. LaPierre produced small silver pieces. It was purchased by the International Silver Company in 1929.

224

225

226

227

228

229

230

231

232

233. Ash tray, 3½"h. x 5"l. x 3"w., silver plated, made by Meriden Silver Plate Company, c.1930, $50-100.

234. Frame, 2½" x 3½", silver plated, c.1950, $50-100.

**Meriden Silver Plate Company** was established in 1869 in Meriden, Connecticut and was among the original companies to form the International Silver Company in 1898.

239. Money clip, 1³/4", sterling, inscribed *United States Golf Association, Organized 1894*, given to contestants in U.S.G.A. Amateur, 1950's-1960's, $75-125.

235. Golf bag, 6"h., sterling, made by Boyden Minuth Co., inscribed *Mrs. Wallace L. Cook Trophy 1927 Beverly Country Club*, marked Handwrought, $600-800.

236.  Coin purse, 2¼" d., silver plated, c.1900, $250-350.

237.  Match safe, 2¼" d., silver with kid purse, hallmark: Birmingham, 1907, $600-800.

238.  Match safe, 1½" x 2¼", silver plated, inscribed *British Saw Fire Ins. Co.*, golfer enameled on reverse, 1920's, $200-300.

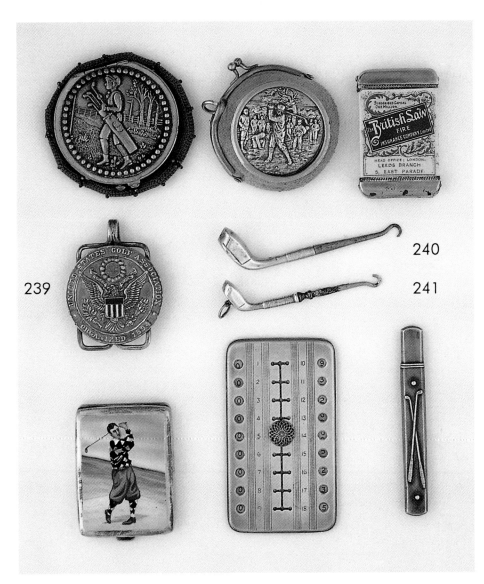

240.  G l o v e hook, 3", silver & steel, unmarked, early 1900's, $75-125.

241.  G l o v e hook, 2½", silver & steel, hallmark: Birmingham, 1908, $75-125.

242.  Match safe, 1¼" x 2³/₈", sterling with new enameling, hallmark: Birmingham, 1926, $75-125.

243.  Score keeper, 2" x 3½", sterling, 1910's, $300-400.

244.  Pencil holder, ½" x 3¼", sterling, 1920's, $100-200.

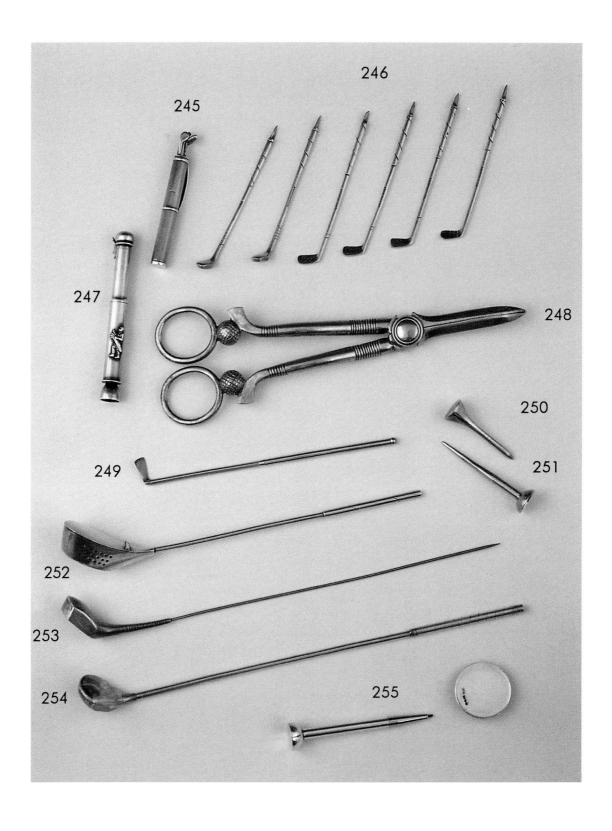

271. Cigarette case, 3¼" x 4½", sterling, enameled, made by Napier Company, Art Deco, c.1930, $400-600.

272. Cigarette case, 3" x 4", sterling, made by The Thomae Co., c.1930, $400-600.

273. Cigarette case, 3" x 4½", sterling, made by Napier Company, Art Deco, c.1930, $300-500.

274. Blotter, 2½" x 4", sterling, made by Unger Bros. (see page 70), c.1905, $800-1200.

The Thomae Co. was initially a division of the Watson Company formed to produce novelties and dresserware developed by Charles Thomae. In 1920, Thomae left Watson and formed Chas. Thomae & Son, which has been managed since his death in 1958 by his two sons.

Napier Company's origins date to 1875, though it was not until 1922 that the name evolved to its current form. Napier has produced primarily jewelry, novelties and dresserware.

**NAPIER**

275.    Cigarette case, 3" x 4", sterling, made by WM. B. Kerr & Co., 1920's, $400-600.

276.    Lady's cigarette case, 3¹/₅" x 3¹/₅", sterling, enameled, marked HAND MADE STERLING, c.1910, $1000-1500.

277.    Cigarette case, 3" x 3½", silver plated, enameled, marked E.C.Co. Nickel Silver, c.1920, $100-200.

278.    Cigarette case, 3" x 4", sterling, enameled, made by Elgin - American Manufacturing Company, c.1920, $500-700.

**Elgin - American Manufacturing Company** was established in 1887 in Elgin, Illinois and produced a variety of silver and silver plated wares. By 1950, Elgin-American was a division of Illinois Watch Case Company.

ELGIN AMERICAN MFG. CO
WARRANTED

279.   Flask, 4" x 8", ⁷/8 pint, sterling, made by WM. B. Kerr & Co., c.1920, $800-1200.

280.   Flask, 4" x 8", ⁷/8 pint, sterling, made by WM. B. Kerr & Co., inscribed *One down and two to go*, c.1920, $800-1200.

**WM. B. Kerr & Co.** was founded in 1855 in Newark, New Jersey, and produced dining and dressing table accessories as well as jewelry. The Gorham Mfg. Co. purchased the firm in 1906, and it was moved to Providence, Rhode Island in 1927.

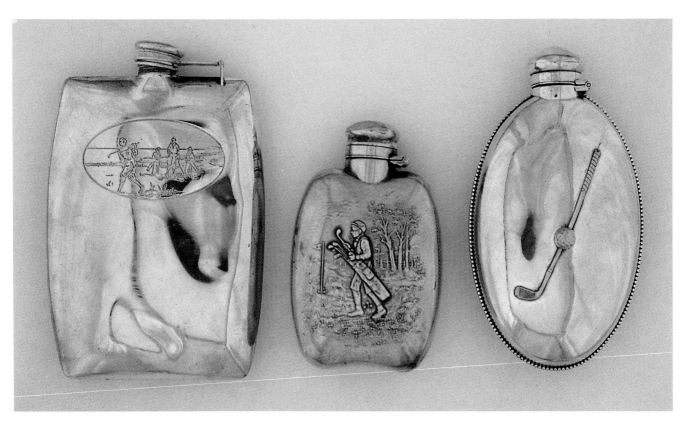

281. Flask, 4" x 6", ½ pint; sterling, made by Watrous Mfg. Co., (see page 75), c.1920, $500-700.

282. Flask, 2½" x 4¼", sterling, made by Unger Bros. (see page 70), c.1905, $1000-1500.

283. Flask, 3¼" x 6", sterling, made by International Silver Co., c.1920, $500-700.

284                    285                    286

309.   Cocktail shaker, tray and 6 cups, pitcher is 13" h., tray 10" x 15", cups 3" h., silver plated, made by Derby Silver Company (see page 87), c.1920, $1500-2000.

310.   Shot glasses, set of four nesting cups in a leather case, 3" h., silver plated, made by Meriden Silver Plate Company (see page 72), 1920's, $250-350.

311.   Place card holders, set of six (two pictured), 1½" d., silver plated, c.1930, $500-700.

312. Trophy, 9" h., sterling, made by Frank M. Whiting, dated 1922, $1000-1500.

313. Trophy, 9" h., sterling, made by Goodnow and Jenks, probably sold by Gorham, c.1910, $800-1200.

314. Trophy, 5" h. plus 3" base, marked sterling 792, inscribed *Oconomowoc Aug 1903*, $500-700.

**Frank M. Whiting Co.** was originally formed as Holbrook, Whiting & Albee in North Attleboro, Massachusetts. The company was called F.M. Whiting in 1878, and Frank M. Whiting Co. in 1896. The firm became a division of Ellmore Silver Co. in 1940 and closed around 1960.

**Goodnow and Jenks** was established as Kennard & Jenks in 1893 in Boston, Massachusetts to manufacture and sell silver products.

**Redlich & Co.** was opened in 1890 as Ludwig, Redlich & Co. by Adolph Ludwig, who sold his interest in 1895. Elgin Silversmith Co. took over the firm in 1946.

337.   Humidor, 7½" h. x 12" l. x 8½" d., silver plated, made by Pairpoint Manufacturing Co., c.1910, $800-1200.

**Pairpoint Manufacturing Company** was organized in 1880 in New Bedford, Massachusetts and named after reknowned artist Thomas Pairpoint, who had previously worked for Gorham and the Meriden Britannia Company. In 1900, Pairpoint merged with Mt. Washington Glass Co. to form the Pairpoint Corporation, which continued operations until 1929.

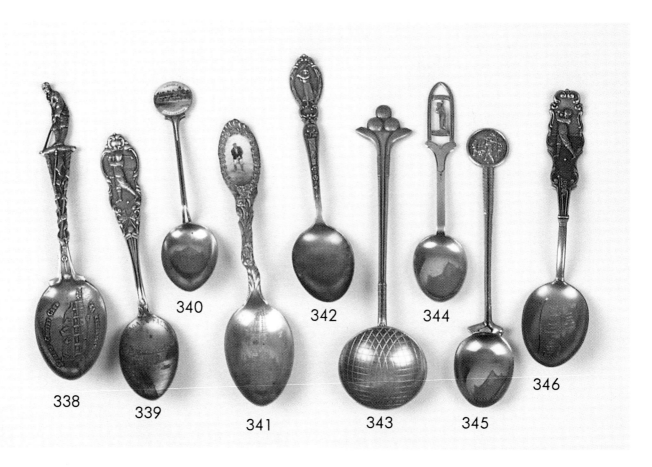

338. Spoon, 6", sterling, made by Mechanics Sterling Company, inscribed *Ekwanok Country Club Manchester VT.*, c.1900, $100-200.

339. Spoon, 5¼", sterling, made by F.S. Gilbert (see page 69), c.1910, $75-125.

340. Spoon, 4¼", sterling, enameled, inscribed *Kingussie Golf Club House*, hallmark: R.C., Birmingham, 1906, $75-125.

341. Spoon, 5½", sterling, enameled, marked S No.26, dated 1920, $200-300.

342. Spoon, 5", sterling, made by Manchester Silver Co., c.1904, $100-200.

343. Spoon, 5¾", sterling, made by Tiffany & Co. (see page 69), c.1925, $200-300.

344. Spoon, 4¼", sterling, hallmark: CU, Chester, 1926, $30-60.

345. Spoon, 5¼", sterling, hallmark: JE, London, 1924, $75-125.

346. Spoon, 5½", sterling, made by Codding Bros. & Heilborn, c.1900, $75-125.

347. Soup ladle, 17", sterling with ivory handle, made by Frank W. Smith Silver Company, dated 1901, $800-1200.

Closeup of #341

Closeup of #345

**Frank W. Smith Silver Company** was established in 1886 in Gardner, Massachusetts, where it produced flatware and holloware in sterling silver until 1958, when the firm was sold to the Webster Company.

**Manchester Silver Company** was established in Providence, Rhode Island in 1887 by William H. Manchester, who came from a family of silversmiths. The company has produced sterling flatware as well as holloware.

**Mechanics Sterling Company** is known to have begun manufacturing flatware in Attleboro, Massachusetts, no later than 1896, as a branch of nearby Watson, Newell Company.

**Codding Bros. & Heilborn** began in 1879 to manufacture silver novelties in North Attleboro, Massachusetts, later expanding into jewelry and silverware. The firm was closed in 1918.

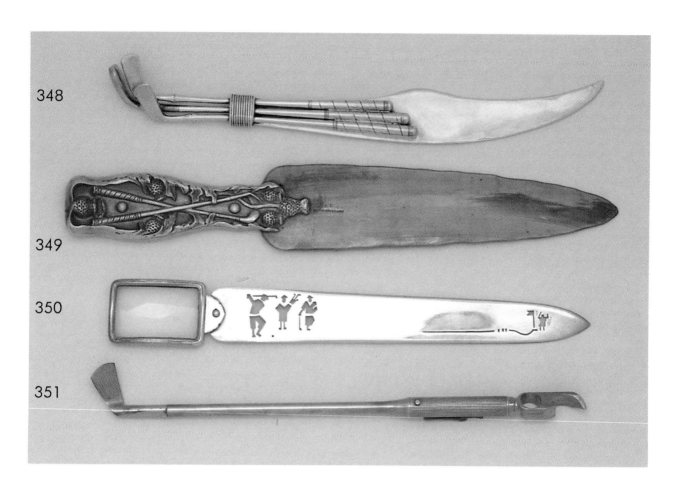

348.   Letter opener, 10½", sterling, made by George W. Shiebler, c.1890, $1200-1800.

349.   Letter opener, 11½", copper & silver, marked Copper and Silver, c.1900, $800-1200.

350.   Letter opener, scene of hole-in-one cut into blade, 10", sterling, marked Cartier Made in France, Art Deco, c.1930, $2000-3000.

351.   Bottle opener & cork screw, 10", silver plated, c.1910, $200-300.

**George W. Shiebler** purchased a New York silver manufacturer which he renamed after himself in 1876. He subsequently bought several other silver firms and incorporated in 1892. The firm went out of business by 1915.

Since 1847, **Cartier** has had a retail operation in Paris which sold jewelry made by their own craftsmen, as well as other wares, made by other manufacturers and marked with the Cartier name.

367.   Figure of Glenna Collette (Vare), 15½" h., bronze, made by Gorham (see page 65), marked E.E. Codman, c.1930, $4500-6500.

368.   Figure, 17" h., bronze with marble base, made in France, signed D. CHAROL, Art Deco, 1920's, $4000-6000.

369.  Bookends, figures of golfer & caddy, 8" h. and 5" h., bronze with marble bases, marked Austria, c.1920, $800-1200.

370.  Figure of a frog, 8" h., bronze, marked J.C. Robert, c.1920, $800-1200.

371.  Figure, 8" h., bronze, c.1930, $600-800.

372.  Ash tray, 6" h., bronze, marked C D M, Art Nouveau, c.1910, $400-600.

373.  Figural ink well, 6" h., bronze, made by Gibbons, marked W'HAMPTON, c.1900, $800-1200.

374. Cigarette holder in the shape of a golf bag, 4", copper with bronze patina, made by Jennings Bros. Mfg. Co., 1930's, $150-250.

375. Figure, swings in the middle, 4" h., metal, c.1930, $200-300.

376. Ash tray, 5 ½" h. x 7" l. x 5" deep, cast iron figure, movable golf ball head, c.1930, $150-250.

377. Bookends (one pictured) with removable golf sticks, 4½" h., metal, c.1930, $150-250.

378. Ash tray, 5" h. x 8" l. x 5" deep, metal figures with stone base, Art Deco, c.1910, $150-250.

**Jennings Bros. Manufacturing Co.** produced mostly silver plated dining and bath accessories in Bridgeport, Connecticut. The trademark JB was used on novelties.

379.    Bookends (one pictured), 5¼" h. x 4" l., cast iron, relief of golfer addressing ball, caddie standing in rear, c.1910, $200-300.

380.    Bookends (one pictured), 4½" h., white metal, 1920's, $150-250.

381.    Bookends (one pictured), 5" h. x 3½" l., bronze, made by Connecticut Foundry Co., inscribed *profanity* under the scene, dated 1928, $100-200.

382.    Ash tray, figure of a woman, 5" h. x 5¼" dia., brass, matches ash tray with figure of a man, item #384, c.1920, $200-300.

383.    Bookends (one pictured), 4" h., brass, marked Art Brass Co. N.Y., c.1920, $200-300.

384.    Ashtray, figure of a man, 5" h. x 5½" dia., brass, matches ashtray with figure of woman, item #382, c.1920, $200-300.

385.   Bookends, 5" h., brass, Art Deco, c.1930, $200-300.

386.   Bookends (one pictured), 6" h., metal, c.1900, $100-200.

387.   Ash tray, 9" h. x 9½" l. x 7" deep, bronze, c.1900, $500-700.

388.   Ash tray, 10" h. x 8" l. x 6" deep, metal on marble base, marked Germany, c.1910, $300-400.

389. Figure, 9" h., nickel plated brass, Art Deco, c.1930, $400-600.

**Byron Nelson** was an extremely successful professional golfer from the 1930's to the 1950's. He won the Masters and the P.G.A. tournaments twice, and the U.S. and French Opens once each. In 1944, he won 13 professional tournaments and in 1945, he won 18 professional tournaments, including 11 in a row.

**C.B. Macdonald** was one of the fathers of golf in America. He designed the first 18-hole golf course in the U.S. in Wheaton, Illinois, and was one of the founders of the Amateur Golf Association of the U.S., later known as the United States Golf Association.

**Bobby Jones** was the winner of more than a dozen U.S. and British Open and Amateur tournaments from 1917 to 1930, including the U.S. Open four times and the U.S. Amateur five times. In 1930, he won the U.S. and British Opens as well as the U.S. and British Amateur titles.

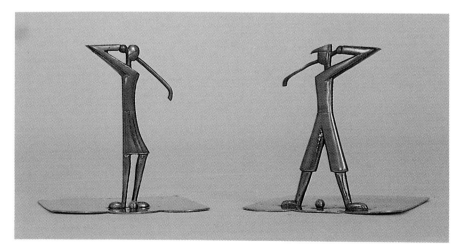

390. Bookends, 4" h., bronze, made by Karl Hagenauer Werkstätte (see page 102), Art Deco, c.1920, $1000-1400.

These three figures were all made of bonded bronze, have a bronze patina and marble base; sculpted by Alfred Petitto in 1988, approximate issue price was $85 each.

391.  Figurine, 9½" h., of Byron Nelson, $100-150.
392.  Figurine, 9 1/8" h., of C.B. Macdonald, $100-150.
393.  Figurine, 8¼" h., of Bobby Jones, $100-150.

394.  Inkwell with pen holder, 3½" h. x 5" l. x 2½" deep, pot metal, c.1940's, $250-350.

395.  Watch holder, 5¾" h. x 3½" l. x 1¾" deep, pot metal, unmarked, late 1920's, $300-400.

396.  Watch holder, 4" h. x 3¼" l. x 2" deep, pot metal, late 1920's, $300-400.

397.  Pipe holder, 4½" h. x 3" dia., pot metal, 1920's, $400-600.

398. Ash tray & match holder, 4½" h., metal, made by Derby Silver Company (see page 87), c.1935, Art Deco, $200-300.

399. Match holder & striker, 4½" h., brass, c.1910, $75-125.

400. Brass pin holder, 3½" l. x 1½" h., 1920's, $100-200.

401. A s h t r a y, 1³/4" h. x 4" d., marked solid pewter, c.1935, $50-100.

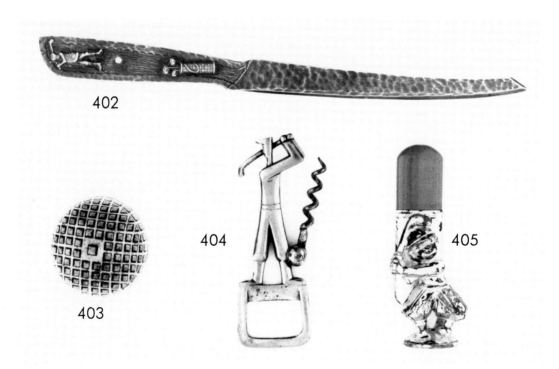

402. Letter opener, 9", bronze, marked MADE BY HAND, 1910's, $150-250.

403. Pencil sharpener in the shape of a mesh golf ball, 1³/4" d., painted metal, marked Germany, 1920's, $30-60.

404. Bottle opener and corkscrew, 3³/4", metal, made in Austria, 1930's, $50-100.

405. C i g a r e t t e lighter, 3½", metal, marked made in Germany, 1930's, $100-200.

407.   Golf ball ice cream mold, 1³/4", pewter,
marked E & Co. NY, c.1910, $100-200.

406. Playing card
case,    2½" x 3½",
brass with black
enamel, late 1920's,
$50-100.

408. Golf bag ice
cream mold, 5¼",
pewter,     marked
Krauss & Son NY,
c.1910, $100-200.

409.   Set of six dress shirt studs with original leather case, ½" d., brass,
enameled, made by Finnigans, c.1900, $600-900.

410   411   412

413   414   415

416   417   418

413.  Hole-in-one medal, 1¼" d., brass, engraved: PRESENTED BY THE MAKERS OF U.S. GOLF BALLS, c.1930, $100-200.

414.  Bag tag, 1" x 1¾", brass, c.1920, $50-100.

415.  Match safe, 2½", brass, c.1900, $150-250.

416.  Match safe, 1½" x 3", aluminum, Art Nouveau, c.1900, $75-125.

417.  Flash light, 1½" x 3", nickel plated brass, c.1920, $50-100.

418.  Cigarette case, 2¼" x 3½", aluminum, c.1900, $100-200.

438.   Box, 8½" l. x 3½" w. x 2½" h., sterling silver on bronze, made by Heintz Art Metal Shop, 1910's, $300-500.

439.   Cigarette box, 3" l. x 4½" w. x 1½" h., brass, marked Acorn Utility Gifts, 1930's, $100-200.

440.   Box with ashtrays inside,   3³/4" l. x 4½" w. x 2" h., bronze, made by Smith Metal Arts Company (see page 125), Art Deco, 1920's, $400-600.

441.   Cigarette box, 7" l. x 3½" w. x 1³/4" h., brass & catalin (similar to plastic), marked Germany, Art Deco, 1920's, $200-300.

442.    Cigarette box, 7½" l. x 4½" w. x 3½" h., sterling silver on bronze, made by Heintz Art Metal Shop (see page 122), 1910's, $400-600.

443.    Cigarette box, 4½" l. x 3½" w. x 2" h., sterling silver on bronze, made by Heintz Art Metal Shop (see page 122), 1910's, $200-300.

444.    Cigarette box, 6" l. x 3½" w. x 1½" h., bronze with sterling silver decoration, made by Smith Metal Arts Company, Art Deco, 1920's, $500-700.

445.    Cigarette box, 3½" l. x 4" w. x 1½" h., bronze with sterling decoration, made by Smith Metal Arts Company, Art Deco, 1920's, $300-450.

446.   Cigarette box, 3½" h. x 4½" d., bronze, made by Smith Metal Arts Company, Art Deco, 1920's, $250-350.

447.   Covered ash tray, 1¼" h. x 4" d., bronze, made by Smith Metal Arts Company, Art Deco, 1920's, $150-250.

**Smith Metal Arts Co.**, of Buffalo, NY, were producers of silver plated, embossed and decorated accessories, primarily desk or smoking items. Established in 1919 by Fred Smith, formerly of Heintz Art Metal Shop, Smith Metal Arts Co.'s Silver Crest trademark was used on works produced during the 1920's.

448.   Weather vane, 72" h. x 90" l., cast iron, 1920's, $3000-5000.

**Hubley Manufacturing Company** had been a cast iron toy manufacturer in Lancaster, Pennsylvania since 1894, and expanded into doorstops and other goods in the 1920's.

449.  Weather vane, 14" h. x 19" l., brass, 1920's, $700-1000.

450.  Doorstop, 8" h., cast iron, made by Hubley Manufacturing Company, 1920's, $300-400.

451.  Doorstop, 8½", cast iron, unknown maker, figure of a black caddy, 1920's, $350-450.

452.   Glass frame, 5½" x 7½", cast iron, marked Germany and as shown below, 1920's, $100-200.

453.   Plaque, 6" d., brass, inscribed *Goodall Tournament*, c.1940, $100-200.

# MECHANICAL DEVICES

Most collectible categories consist of non-functioning items. Some exceptions exist, including watches, mechanical banks and cigarette lighters.

The combination of a golf design and an inexpensive watch movement can result in a much higher value to a decorative golf collector than a watch collector would consider reasonable.

454. Clock, 5" x 5", marble with silver golf sticks and hand painted face, marked CH Hour France, Art Deco, 1930's, $1000-1500.

455. Clock, 6½" x 6½, silver plated, made by J.E. Caldwell & Co., Art Deco, c.1930, $700-1000.

456

457

458

459

460

461

462

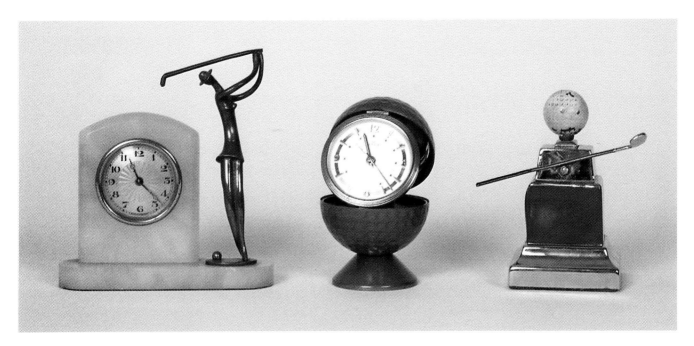

463. Clock, 5½" h. x 5" l., marble & bronze, figure is signed Hagenauer (see page 102), Art Deco, c.1930, $1000-1500.

464. Clock, 4¼" h. when open, brass, made by Rensie, c.1950, $40-80.

465. Lighter, 4½" h., metal, Art Deco, 1930's, $200-300.

456. Wristwatch, 1" d., 9 karat gold case, marked Swiss Dunlop, late 1920's, $1000-1500.

457. Wrist watch, 1¼" d., gold plated top, made by Elgin-American Manufacturing Company (see page 80), 1930's, $400-600.

458. Watch in a golf ball, 1¼" d., metal, marked Mido Limited 17 Jewels, new dial marked Mathey Tissot, c.1930, $500-700.

459. Pocket watch, 1½" d., silver plated, made by Talis, marked Brev.+Dem Swiss Made, c.1920, $600-800.

460. Pocket watch, 1½" d., brass case with white enamel, made by Intex, marked 17 Rubis, c.1940, $150-250.

**Tiffany & Co.** made watch cases, but did not manufacture the rest of the watch, though at times the face was marked Tiffany.

461. Pocket watch, 1½" d., sterling, enameled, made by Abra, Art Deco, 1930's, $500-700.

462. Pocket watch, 1¼" d., .935 sterling case, case made by Tiffany & Co., Art Nouveau, c.1900, $1200-1800.

466.   Clock, 9" h. x 9½" l., metal, c.1900, $600-800.

467.  Lamp,  18"  h., glass & metal, c.1940, $300-400.

468.   Thermometer, 7" h., white metal, dark brown patina, marked Thermo-o-dial, c.1910, $200-300.

469.   Bank, 6" h. x 9" l. x 3½" deep, cast iron, probably made in the 1950's, $300-500; a similar version is being made currently, retail around $30.

# GRAPHICS & MISCELLANEOUS

This chapter includes an assortment of collectibles with golf motifs, made from materials including silk, wood, paper, cardboard and tin.

Many of these, as well as other pieces shown in this book, were created with advertising or promotional purposes in mind. Golf has long been portrayed as the sport of rich, sophisticated men and women. Images of golfers and golfing have been used to enhance the desirability of products or services in a range of areas, most prominently among alcohol and tobacco related products, but extending to a diverse group of products, from cuff links to Coca-Cola.

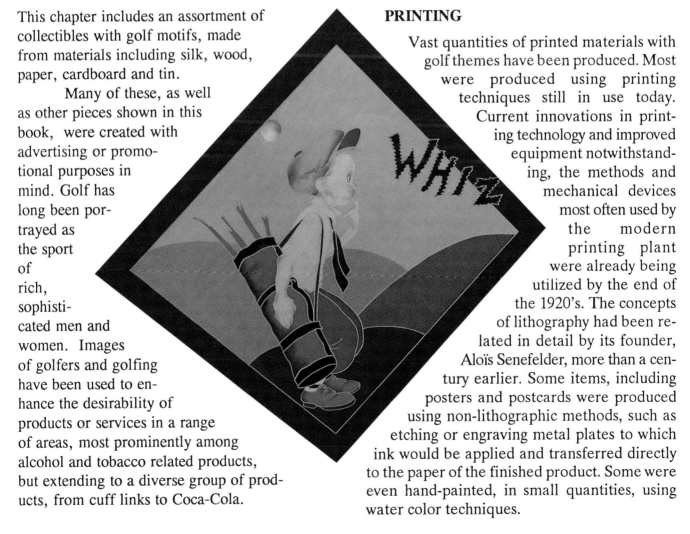

470. Scarf, framed, 34" x 34", silk, Art Deco, c.1930, $1000-1400.

## PRINTING

Vast quantities of printed materials with golf themes have been produced. Most were produced using printing techniques still in use today. Current innovations in printing technology and improved equipment notwithstanding, the methods and mechanical devices most often used by the modern printing plant were already being utilized by the end of the 1920's. The concepts of lithography had been related in detail by its founder, Aloïs Senefelder, more than a century earlier. Some items, including posters and postcards were produced using non-lithographic methods, such as etching or engraving metal plates to which ink would be applied and transferred directly to the paper of the finished product. Some were even hand-painted, in small quantities, using water color techniques.

471. Tray, 10½" x 19", wood, c.1930, $400-600.

472. Plaque, 6" x 9", wood, c.1935, $150-250.

473. Handkerchief box, 9½" x 9½", wood, c.1930, $100-200.

474.   Tray, 13½" x 19½", sterling silver under glass and wood frame, c.1920, $700-1000.

475.   Lawn & house golf game, 3" h. x 41" l. x 10" deep, wood, made by B. Perkins & Son, marked Simpson's Patent, c.1890, $1200-1800.

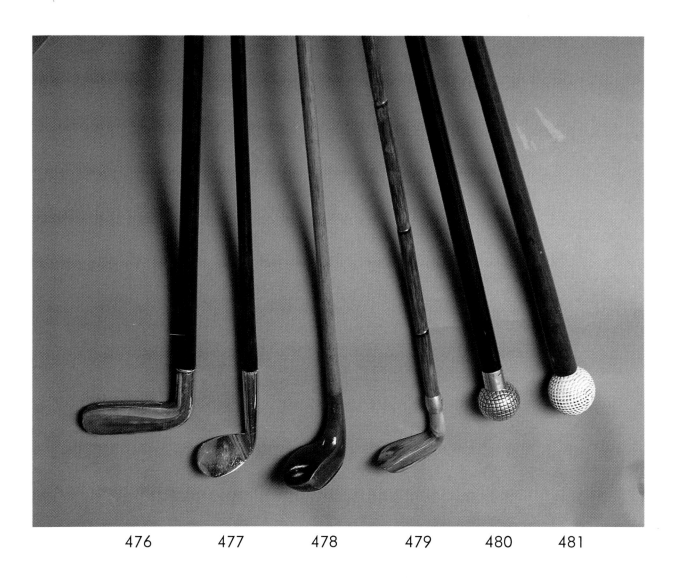

476      477      478      479      480      481

476. Cane, 36" l., handle opens to hold cigarettes, wood with 800 silver handle, c.1920, $600-900.

477. Cane, 37" l., wood with cast head made from a rut iron, originally produced by James Hutchison of North Berwick (1847-1912), and nickel plated for use as a cane head, c.1890, $600-800.

478. Cane, 33" l., wood, probably for a woman, head is a replica of early wood, including fiber sole plate and lead weight, c.1900, $300-400.

479. Cane, 34" l., bamboo with horn head and sterling ferrule, engraved BBF Bangor ME, c.1900, $300-400.

480. Cane, 37" l., wood with sterling handle, made by CC, engraved Brigg, hallmark: London, 1892, engraved Seton Guthrie from Toomey, $600-900.

481. Cane, 35" l., wood, c.1910, $400-600.

483.   Smoking stand, 27" h., metal, made by Porceloid Products Inc., Art Deco, c.1928, $300-500.

484.   Fireplace poker, 25" h., brass, 1950's, $300-500.

482.   Putter with sterling silver head, 37" l., made by Probst, U.S.A., marked West Point and Dyna Weight, 1950's, $800-1200.

Close-up of #486.

483          484

485.   Putter, 35" l., wood shaft with sterling head, made by Lambert Bros. Jewelers, marked Walter Hagen, Putter, c.1930, $1200-1800.

486.   Golf stick, 41" l., wood with silver plated head & ferrule, ferrule engraved A Coste Souvenir du Golf de Handi Novembre 1929 R. Daurelle P Bernhard Hilaire Chicette et Mado M Bruneliere T Hibon, and carved dragon, c.1929, $1000-1500.

487. **Second Shots: Casual Talks about Golf**, by Bernard Darwin, published in London by George Newnes, Ltd., 1930, 178 pages, 6⅝" x 5¼".

488. **Locker Room Ballads**, by W. Hastings Webling, published in Toronto by S.B. Gundy, 1925, 95 pages, 7¾" x 5¼".

489. **'Carry Your Bag, Sir?' A History of Golf's Caddies**, by David Stirk, published in London by H. F. & G. Witherby Ltd., 1989, 128 pages, 8½" x 6".

490. **Collecting Old Golfing Clubs**, by Alick A. Watt, published in Alton Hants, England by A.A. Watt & Son, 1985, 119 pages, 8½" x 6".

491. **Triumphant Journey: The Saga of Bobby Jones and the Grand Slam of Golf**, by Dick Miller, published in New York by Holt, Rinehart and Winston, 1980, 258 pages, 9¼" x 6¼".

492. **Our Lady of the Green (A Book of Ladies Golf)**, by L. Mackern and M. Boys, published in London by Lawrence and Bullen, Ltd., 1899, 7½" x 5".

493. **Drives and Puts: A Book of Golf Stories**, by Walter Camp and Lillian Brooks, published in Boston by L.C. Page and Company, 1899, 243 pages, 7¼" x 4¾".

494. **The Life of Tom Morris; with Glimpses of St. Andrews and Its Golfing Celebrities**, by W.W. Tulloch, D.D., published in London by T. Werner Laurie, c.1908, 334 pages, 9" x 6⅛".

495. **Muirfield and The Honourable Company**, by George Pottinger, published in Edinburgh by Scottish Academic Press, 1972, 146 pages, 9½" x 6¼".

496. **Golf: Pleasures of Life Series**, by Bernard Darwin, published in London by Burke, 1954, 222 pages, 8⅞" x 5¾".

497. **So This is Golf!**, by Harry Leon Wilson, published in New York by Cosmopolitan Book Corporation, 1923, 46 pages, 7½" x 5⅛".

498. **On Many Greens: A Book of Golf and Golfers**, by Miles Bantock, published in New York by Grosset & Dunlap, 1901, 167 pages, 7" x 4⅝".

499. **The Soul of Golf**, by P.A. Vaile, published in London by Macmillan and Co., Ltd., 1912, 356 pages, 8" x 5⅜".

500. **The Golfer's Manual**, by W. Meredith Butler, published in London by T. Werner Laurie, c.1907, 171 pages, 7⅝" x 5⅛".

501. **Golf Without Tears**, by P. G. Wodehouse, published in New York by A.L. Burt Company, c.1924, 330 pages, 7⅝" x 5⅛".

502. **Golf For Women**, by Genevieve Hecker, published in New York by The Baker & Taylor Company, c.1904, 217 pages, 8½" x 5¾".

---

Note: There are many variables which influence the value of books, including the edition, type of cover, presence or lack of a dust jacket, author's signature and condition. We have not included values of books in **Decorative Golf Collectibles** because of the difficulty in providing values useful for purposes of comparison to those books you may find.

503. **A History of Golf: The Royal and Ancient Game**, by Robert Browning, published in London by J.M. Dent, 1955, 236 pages, 8⁷/₈" x 6¼".

504. **The Art of Golf**, by Sir W.G. Simpson, Bart., published in Edinburgh by David Douglas, 1887, 186 pages, 8⁷/₈" x 5³/₄".

505. **Golf Architecture in America: Its Strategy and Construction**, by George C. Thomas, Jr., published in Los Angeles, CA by The Times Mirror Press, 1927, 9" x 6³/₈".

506. **Poems on Golf**, by Robert Clark, published in Edinburgh, printed for private circulation, 1867, 78 pages, 9³/₈" x 7".

507. **The Rules of Golf of the Ten Oldest Golf Clubs from 1754 to 1848 Together with the Rules of the Royal & Ancient Golf Club of St. Andrews for the Years 1858, 1875, 1888**, by C.B. Clapcott, published in Edinburgh by Golf Monthly, 1935, 127 pages, 8⁵/₈" x 5⁵/₈".

508. **Some Essays on Golf Course Architecture**, by Harry S. Colt & C.H. Alison, published in London by Country Life & George Newnes, 1920, 69 pages, 7½" x 5¹/₈".

509. **Collecting Golf Books, 1743-1938**, by Cecil Hopkinson, published in London by Constable and Co., Ltd., 1938, 56 pages, 7⁵/₈" x 5¹/₈".

510. **On The Links, Being Golfing Stories by Various Hands, with Shakespeare on Golf, By a Novice**, by William Angus Knight, published in Edinburgh by David Douglas, 1899, 63 pages, 7¹/₈" x 5".

511. **Golf in America; A Practical Manual**, by James P. Lee, published in New York by Dodd, Mead & Co., 1895, 194 pages, 6⁷/₈" x 4¼"; first golf book printed in the United States.

512. **Fifty years of American Golf**, by H.B. Martin, published in New York by Dodd, Mead & Co., 1936, 423 pages, 9½" x 7".

## PRINTING TECHNIQUES

Lithography has been the most popular method for reproducing graphic artwork since the early 1900's. The handwork techniques (besides creating the design) which will be described here have been replaced for the most part by photomechanical methods of reproduction. What makes lithography possible is the fact that grease attracts grease and repels water.

In the early days of lithography, designs were produced using a greasy crayon, made of soap, wax, oil and lampblack. The designs were originally made on stone. Paper was later used as the design base, to be transferred to a zinc or aluminum plate. The design was coated with a mixture of acid and gum arabic. The gum arabic kept the non-design area free from grease and the acid eliminated any stray grease in those areas. The design was protected from the acid by the wax in the crayon in which it was drawn. The crayon was then washed off, but in its place, the plate absorbed oil which would preserve the design. When water was applied, it adhered only to the non-design area, being repelled by the grease in the design areas of the plate. When ink was then applied, it was attracted only to the design areas in which grease was present. The ink was composed of dry color and linseed oil.

Before 1864, lithography involved only black ink, but after that, multiple colors were used in some designs. One plate was needed for each color of ink to be used. At the time, each color had to be printed individually, dried and then the process repeated. By 1929, presses were available to print two, three and four colors at a time. To be exact, each individual sheet was imprinted by one plate followed immediately by the next plate, and so on, each inked with a different color.

The printing machines used in the early 1900's included a hand-press used for making proofs and for printing very small numbers of copies. The power driven flat-bed machine was used primarily for printing from stone, and naturally gave way to the direct rotary and offset machines. because stone was so unweildy relative to metal plates. The direct rotary machine was far faster than the flat-bed, and consisted of two cylinders, one to carry the plate with the design and one to supply the pressure needed to transfer the ink from plate to paper. Pictorial posters were largely printed using the direct rotary machine.

Offset presses differed from direct rotary presses in much the way their name describes. Whereas the rotary machine required direct contact between plate and paper, the offset press had a third cylinder covered with a sheet of rubber, onto which the inked design from the plate cylinder was transferred, and from which the ink was then trans-

---

516.   **A History of the Royal & Ancient Golf Club, St. Andrews From 1754-1900**, by H.S.C. Everard, published in Edinburgh & London by William Blackwood and Sons, 1907, 306 pages, 10¼" x 7 ⁷/₈".

517.   **Golf: The Badminton Library of Sports and Pastimes**, published in London by Longmans, Green and Co., 1890, 495 pages, 9⁷/₈" x 7⁷/₈"; large paper edition limited to 250 copies.

518.   **The Architectural Side of Golf**, by H.N. Wethered and T. Simpson, published in London by Longman, Green and Co., 1929, 211 pages, 10" x 7³/₄".

519.   **Chronicles of Blackheath Golfers, with Illustrations and Portraits**, by W.E. Hughes, published in London by Chapman and Hall, Limited, 1897, 245 pages, 10" x 7⁷/₈".

520.   **The Royal and Ancient Game of Golf**, by Harold H. Hilton and Garden C. Smith, published in London by Golf Illustrated and The London and Counties Press Assoc. Ltd., 1912, 276 pages, 12½" x 10½"; this edition is limited to 900 copies.

521.   **British Golf Links; A Short Account of the Leading Golf Links of the United Kingdom**, by Horace Hutchinson, published in London by J.S. Virtue & Co., Ltd., 1897, 331 pages, 13" x 10".

ferred to the paper. Offset is especially suitable for printing on surfaces which are not perfectly uniform, such as uncoated paper, fabric, leather, and tin. The resiliency of the rubber allows ink to reach areas of the printing surface which might be slightly depressed relative to the highest points on the surface. Thus, the image is transferred more uniformly to all areas of the receiving material.

Offset was used to print on sheets of tin destined to become tin containers, even before it was used to print on paper. After the design was transferred to the prepared sheet of tin, the sheet was dried at a high temperature, the process being repeated once for each color used in the design.

The state of the art in printing at the end of the 1920's was such that we are today employing much the same basic technology, albeit with greater precision and speed. The development of photo-mechanical methods had by that time made possible the reproduction of continuous tones (shades of colors, or shades of gray between white and black), by "screening" the original photographic image to convert it to a pattern of dots of varying sizes. Black dots in the correct pattern appear as shades of gray which vary according to their size and concentration. Dots of cyan (blue), magenta (red), yellow and black can be utilized to create the impression of the spectrum of colors. "It was not uncommon under the old method, when reproducing a colour printing, to have as many as 20 printings, each of a different colour or tint. The modern method (a photo-mechanical one) whereby colour negatives are secured by scientific photographic dissection of the colours of an original, has been made possible by the development of photography and the progress of mechanical science." [*Graphic Arts*, p.68] This is now known as color separation, and the wording may be antiquated, but the concepts on which modern printing is based, were for the most part already understood and being utilized over 60 years ago.

---

**522. The Story of American Golf, Its Champions and Its Championships,** by Herbert Warren Wind, published in New York by Farrar, Straus and Company, 1948, 502 pages, 11¼" x 8½".

**523. A History of Golf in Britain,** by Bernard Dawin and others, published in London by Cassell & Company, Ltd., 1952, 312 pages, 11¹/8" x 8 ¼".

**524. Scotland's Gift, Golf: Reminiscences 1872-1927,** by Charles Blair Macdonald, published in New York by Charles Scribner's Sons, 1928, 340 pages, 10½" x 8".

**525. The Golf Book of East Lothian,** by John Kerr, M.A., F.R.S.E., F.S.A. Scot., Minister of Dirleton, published in Edinburgh by T. and A. Constable, 1896, 516 pages plus 34 page appendix, 10" x 7³/4"; this is the small paper edition limited to 500 copies.

**526. The Golf Courses of the British Isles,** by Bernard Darwin, published in London by Duckworth & Co., 1910, 254 pages, 9¼" x 7 ³/8".

**527. The Life of Tom Morris; with Glimpses of St. Andrews and Its Golfing Celebrities,** by W.W. Tulloch, D.D., published in London by T. Werner Laurie, c.1908, 334 pages, 9" x 6¹/8".

528. Post card, 4" x 6", paper, signed Louis Baumer, c.1920, $50-100.

**Rene Vincent** was a popular French graphic artist and illustrator known for Art Deco fashion and automobile posters.

529. Post card, 4" x 6", paper, signed Rene Vincent, c.1930, $50-100.

530. Poster, 25" x 40", paper, by Lucien Serre & Co. Paris, signed P. Pommarmond, c.1930, $1000-1500.

531. Post card, 4" x 6", paper, signed Mollie Benatar, c.1920, $50-100.

532. Post card, 4" x 6", paper, Art Deco, c.1920, $50-100.

533. Post card, 4" x 6", paper, signed Rene Vincent, c.1930, $50-100.

534. Post card, 4" x 6", paper, signed B. B. Macklin, c.1920, $50-100.

535.   Golf ball box, 2" h. x 7³/₄" l. x 6" w., wood, c. 1900, $300-400.

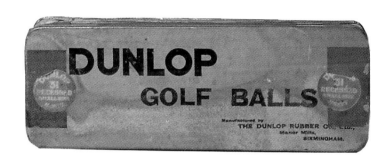

536.   Cigar tin, 5½" h. x 5" l. x 5" d., 1920's, $300-400.

537.   Golf ball box, 2" h. x 10½" l. x 3³/₄" d., tin, c.1915, $300-500.

538.   Golf ball box, 7¼" x 5½", cardboard, Worthington Ball Co., Elyria, OH, 1932, $50-100.

539.   Golf ball tin, 7¼" x 5½", St. Mungo Manufacturing Company, Govan Scotland, c.1909, $500-700.

540        541                    542                    543

544. Coca Cola tray, 13¼" x 10½", tin, made in 1926, $500-700.

545. Biscuit can, 10¾" h. x 3¼" d., tin, painted, by Robertson Bros. Ltd., Toronto & London, 1920's, $350-500.

540.   Advertising sign, 13½" x 12", cardboard, 1920's, $50-100.

541.   Box with whipping, 7½" x 7½", cardboard, P. Stewart & Sons, *Pitched Golf Thread*, Lisburn N. Ireland, c.1910, $200-300.

542.   Box, 5¼" x 6¼", cardboard, *Wilson Putting Disc., The Putting Instructor*, 1940's, $20-40.

543.   Box, 4" h. x 3" l. x 1" deep, cardboard, front reads: *The Ri-Co. Muffler*, back reads N.J. Rich & Co., Cleveland, Ohio, dated 1911, $20-40.

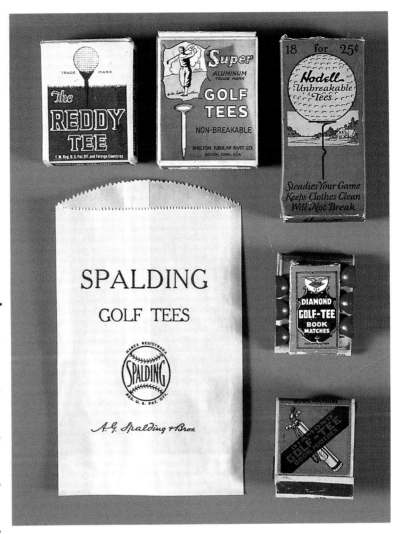

546.   Package, 2" x 2½", cardboard, *The Reddy Tee*, 1920's, under $20.

547.   Package, 2" x 2³/4", cardboard, *Super Golf Tees*, 1920's, $20-40.

548.   Package, 1½" x 3½", cardboard, *Hadell Tees*, 1920's, $20-40.

549.   Paper bag, 6½" x 4", *Spalding Tees*, c.1910, $20-40.

550.   Tee and match holder, 1½" x 2", cardboard, *Diamond Golf Tees & Matches*, early 1920's, under $20.

551.   Sponge (golf ball cleaner), 2¼" x 2", tin case, c.1930's-1940's, $20-40.

552.   Package of razor blades (front and back shown), 2" x 1", cardboard, *Golf Blade Co.*, 1933, under $20.

553.   Matches, 1½" x 2", cardboard, *Po Do matches*, 1940's, under $10.

554.   Compact, *Outdoor Girl Face Powder*, 1⁵/8" diameter, tin, late 1930's, under $20.

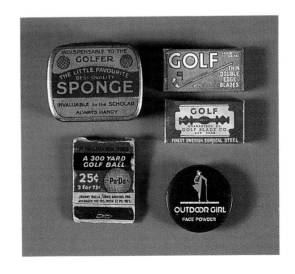

555. Playing cards, made by Americas Playing Cards, early 1900's, $40-80.

556. Playing cards, gilt edges, *Golf Belle*, made by Standard Playing Cards, early 1900's, $50-100.

557. Pad holder, 4"x 2½", leather, sold in Sebring FL, 1910's, $50-100.

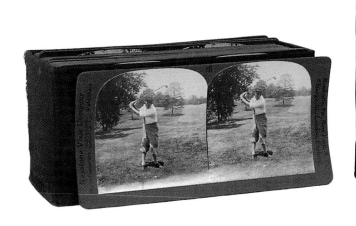

558. Stereo views, set of 50 views of famous players, commentary by Grantland Rice, 6"x 3" images, paper, by Keystone View Co., late 1920's, $900-1200.

# BIBLIOGRAPHY

## General

Baddiel, Sarah, 1898. *Golf: The Golden Years*, Chartwell Books, Inc., Secaucus, New Jersey.

Duncan, Alastair, 1986. *American Art Deco*, Abrams, New York.

Kirsner, Gary and Gruhl, Jim, 1990. *The Beer Stein Book*, Glentiques, Ltd., Coral Springs, Florida.

Marion, John L., ed., 1989-1990 . *Sotheby's International Price Guide*, Vendome Press, New York.

Ohlman, John M. and Morton, 1985. *The Encyclopedia of Golf Collectibles*, Books Americana, Florence, Alabama.

Stirk, David, 1987. *Golf: The History of an Obsession*, Phaidon Press, Oxford.

## Ceramics

Bagdade, Susan D. and Allen D., 1987. *Warman's English & Continental Pottery & Porcelain*, Warman Publishing Co., Inc., Willow Grove, Pennsylvania.

Boger, Louise Ade, 1971. *The Dictionary of World Pottery and Porcelain, From Prehistoric Times to the Present*, Charles Scribner's Sons, New York.

Cameron, Elisabeth, 1986. *Encyclopedia of Pottery & Porcelain: 1800-1960*, Facts on File Publications, New York.

Chaffers, William. *Collectors' Handbook of Marks & Monograms on Pottery & Porcelain*, Borden Publishing Company, Alhambra, California.

*Encyclopedia of World Art*, Volume VI. McGraw-Hill Book Company, Inc., London, 1962.

Evans, Paul, 1987. *Art Pottery of the United States*, Feingold & Lewis Publishing Corp., New York.

Fox, Ron and Wald, Mike, September, 1986. "Steins by O'Hara Dial Co." in *Prosit*, Stein Collectors International, Kingston, New Jersey.

Irvine, Louise, 1980. *Royal Doulton Series Ware, Volume I,* Richard Dennis, London.

Irvine, Louise, 1984. *Royal Doulton Series Ware, Volume II,* Richard Dennis, London.

Irvine, Louise, 1984. *Royal Doulton Bunnykins*, Richard Dennis, London.

Kovel, Ralph M. and Terry H., 1953. *Dictionary of Marks: Pottery and Porcelain*, Crown Publishers, Inc., New York.

Kovel, Ralph M. and Terry H., 1961. *A Directory of American Silver, Pewter and Silver Plate*, Crown Publishers, Inc., New York.

Kovel, Ralph M. and Terry H., 1986. *Kovel's New Dictionary of Marks*, Crown Publishers, Inc., New York.

Lehner, Lois. *Lehner's Encyclopedia of U.S. Marks on Pottery, Porcelain & Clay*, Collector Books, Paducah, Kentucky.

Lima, Paul J. and Candace A., 1971. *The Enchantment of Hand Painted Nippon Porcelain*, Silverado Studios, Silverado, California.

Lowenstein, Jack G., June, 1983. "Those Magical Marks" in *Prosit*, Stein Collectors International, Kingston, New Jersey.

Lukins, Jocelyn. "Kings, Queens and Other Wares" in *Royal Doulton International Collectors Club Magazine.*, London.

"Teeing Off with Doulton", Autumn, 1990. *Royal Doulton International Collectors Club Magazine.*, London.

Weiss, Princess and Barry, 1987. *The Original Price Guide to Royal Doulton Discontinued Character Jugs*, Harmony Press, Inc., New York.

Zadra, Frank. "A Collectors World" in *Royal Doulton International Collectors Club Magazine*, London.

Zühlsdorff, Dieter, 1988. *Marken Lexikon: Porzellan und Keramik Report*, Arnold'schen Verlagsanstalt GmbH, Stuttgart, Germany.

## Glass

Farrar, Estelle and Spillman, Jane, 1979. *The Complete Cut & Engraved Glass of Corning*, Crown Publishers, Inc., New York.

Grover, Ray and Lee, 1967. *Art Glass Nouveau*, Charles E. Tuttle Company, Inc, Tokyo.

Jones-North, Jacquelyne Y., 1990. *Czechoslovakian Perfume Bottles and Boudoir Accessories*, Antique Publications, Marietta, Ohio.

Klein, Dan and Lloyd, Ward, eds., 1984. *The History of Glass*, Orbis Publishing, Ltd., London.

National Cambridge Society, 1976. *Colors in Cambridge*, Collector Books, Paducah, Kentucky.

Neuwirth, Waltraud, 1986. *Loetz Austria 1900*, Selbstverlag Dr. Waltraud Neuwirth, Vienna.

Padgett, Leonard E., 1976. *American Cut Glass of the Brilliant Period*, Clinton, Maryland.

Papert, Emma. *The Illustrated Guide to American Glass*, Hawthorn Books, Inc., New York.

Revi, Albert Christian, 1968. *American Art Nouveau Glass*, Thomas Nelson Inc., Nashville, Tennessee.

**Bronze & Other Metals**

Bertoia, Jeanne, 1985. *Doorstops*, Collectors Books, Paducah, Kentucky.

Catley, Bryan, 1978. *Art Deco and other Figures*, Antique Collectors' Club, Woodbridge, Suffolk, England.

Faulkner, Trevor. *The Thames and Hudson Manual of Direct Metal Sculpture*, Thames and Hudson, Ltd., London.

Petretti, Allan, 1989. *Petretti's Coca-Cola Collectibles Price Guide*, Wallace-Homestead Book Company, Radnor, Pennsylvania.

Rich, Jack C., 1947. *The Materials and Methods of Sculpture*, Oxford University Press, New York.

Turner, Eric, 1982. *Brass*, Stemmer House Publishers Inc., Owing Mills, Maryland.

White, Dave, 1987. "A Nearly Forgotten Maker of Memories" in *Homefront,* Buffalo Evening News, Sunday Magazine.

White, Dave, 1987. "Another Metal Shop Makes its Mark Here" in *Homefront*, Buffalo Evening News, Sunday Magazine.

**Silver & Gold**

Banister, 1970. *English Silver Hallmarks*, Wallace Homestead Book Co., Des Moines, Iowa.

Bradbury, Frederick, 1982. *Bradbury's Book of Hallmarks*, J.W. Northend, Ltd., Sheffield, England.

Carpenter, Charles H. and Mary Grace, 1978. *Tiffany Silver*, Dodd, Mead & Company, New York.

Carpenter, Charles H. and Zapata, Janet, 1987. *The Silver of Tiffany & Co..*, Museum of Fine Arts, Boston, Massachusetts.

Rainwater, Dorothy T., 1986. *Encyclopedia of American Silver Manufacturers, Third Edition*, Schiffer Publishing Ltd., West Chester, Pennsylvania.

Rainwater, Dorothy T., 1973. *Sterling Silver Holloware*, The American Historical Catalog Collection, Scribners, New York.

**Graphics**

*Graphic Arts*, 1929. Garden City Publishing Company, New York.

## CATALOGS

Richard E. Donovan Enterprises, The Game of Golf and the Printed Word.

Richard W. Oliver, Inc., Golf Auction.

Kevin C. McGrath, Sporting Antiquities.

Phillips Fine Art Auctioneers, Golfing Memorabilia.

Sotheby's Golf and Sporting Memorabilia.

Christie's Scotland Ltd., Early Golf Equipment, Memorabilia, Pictures and Related Items.

# Ceramics

 Amphora Pottery Works

 Bunnykins [Royal Doulton]

 Burgess & Leigh

 Ceramic Art Company

 Copeland - Spode

Crown Devon [S. Fielding & Co., Ltd.]

 Crown Staffordshire China Co., Ltd.

Dartmouth Pottery, Ltd.

 Dickensware [Weller Pottery]

 Foley China Co.

 Simon Peter Gerz

 Hauber & Reuther

 Lenox China Company

 Lladro

 MacIntyre

 New York & Rudolstadt Pottery

 Nippon

 Noritake

 O'Hara Dial Company

 A.G. Richardson & Co.

 Robinson Clay Products Company

 Robj, Paris

 Rookwood Pottery

  Rosenthal

  Royal Bonn

 Royal Copenhagen Porcelain Factory

 Royal Doulton

 Viktor Schreckengost

 Taylor, Smith & Taylor Company

 Taylor - Tunnecliffe

 A.J. Thewalt

 Wiltshaw & Robinson

# Glass

 De Passe Manufacturing Company

 The Handel Company

 Heinrich Hoffman

 Wave Crest [C.F. Monroe Company]

# Silver, Bronze & Other

 James E. Blake Company

 Codding Bros. & Heilborn

 Derby Silver Company

 F.S. Gilbert

 Goodnow and Jenks

 Gorham

 STERLING   La Pierre Mfg. Co.

 Manchester Silver Company

 Joseph Mayer & Bros.

 Mechanics Sterling Company

 Meriden Silver Plate Company

 Pairpoint Manufacturing Company

Karl Hagenauer Werkstätte

 John Hasselbring

 Redlich & Co.

Heintz Art Metal Shop

 George W. Schiebler

International Silver Company

 Silver Crest
[Smith Metal Arts Co.]

WM. B. Kerr & Co.

Frank W. Smith
Silver Company

The Thomae Co.

Unger Bros.

Watrous Mfg. Co.

Webster Company

Frank M. Whiting Co.

Wilcox Silver Plate
Company

# INDEX

Index 159

Noritake Company, 38, 42, 43
O'Hara Dial Co., 14, 15
Pairpoint Corporation, 59, 95
Patina, 99
Pentunse, 9
Perkins, B. & Son, 135
Perrier, 26
Petitto, Alfred, 113
Pillsbury, Hester, 20
Pommarmond, P., 144
Porcelain, 9
Porceloid Products, 137
Pot metal, 99, 101
Pottery, 9
Printing, 141, 143
Probst, 137
Ransbottom Brothers, 45
Redlich & Co., 90, 91
Reed & Barton, 76, 121
Relief, 12
Rensie, 131
Reproduction, 12, 13, 51, 64, 101
Richardson, A.G. & Co. Ltd., 36
Ridgemoor Country Club, 69
Riessner, 34
Robinson Clay Products Co., 45
Robj, 11
Rogers, 36
Rookwood Pottery, 42, 43
Rosenthal, 45
Royal Bonn, 14, 19
Royal Bradwell, 46
Royal Copenhagen Porcelain Factory, 37
Royal Doulton, 13, 24-32, 43, 47, 48, *see also*
        *Bunnykins, Series Wares*
Royal Worcester, 42
Rules of golf, 26, 28
Saltglaze, 9
Schrekengost, Victor, 33
Schuman, G.A., 75
Schwarzburg, 39
Scotscraig Golf House, 39
Senefelder, Aloïs, 133
Series Wares, 25-27, 29-32, 45
        Gibson Series Ware, 25, 30
        Proverb Series Ware, 25, 31
        Uncle Toby Series Ware, 25, 45
        Golf Series Ware, 26-27, 32, 37
        Golfers Series Ware, 25, 29, 31

Sèvres, 11, 12
Sgraffito, 11, 20
Sheffield Silver Co., 121
Shiebler, George W., 98
Shinnecock Hills Golf Club, 59
Silver, 50, 63, 64
Silver Crest, 125
Silver plating, 63
Skinner & Co., 75
Slip casting, 11
Slip, 11, 12
Smith, Frank W. Silver Company, 97
Smith Metal Arts Company, 119, 123-125
Spencer, 103
Steuben Glass Works, 56
Storer, Maria Longworth Nichols, 42
Stoneware, 9
Swiss Dunlop, 131
Talis, 131
Taylor, Smith & Taylor Company, 32-33, 38
Taylor-Tunnecliffe, 36
Textron, Inc., 65
Thewalt, A.J., 48
Thomae Co., 79
Tiffany & Co., 64, 69, 84, 91, 92, 96
Tiffany, Charles Lewis, 69
Tin, 99, 101, 133, 143
Transfer printing, 12
Udall & Ballou, 94
Unger Bros., 64, 70, 75, 76, 79, 82, 83, 88
United States Golf Association (U.S.G.A.), 72, 112
Upper Montclair Country Club, 67
Venner, Victor, 44
Villeroy & Boch, 19
Vincent, Rene, 144
Walker & Hall, 86, 87
Warwick China Company, 44, 45
Watches, 129
Watrous Mfg. Co., 75, 76, 82
Wave Crest Ware, 58
Webster Company, 76, 97
Weller Pottery, 20
Weller, Samuel A., 20
Wheaton, 121
Whiting, Frank M., 64, 90
Wilcox Silver Plate Co., 83-85
Wileman & Co., 39, 43
Wiltshaw & Robinson, 35, 38
Winarick, AR Co., 61

# OTHER TITLES AVAILABLE FROM GLENTIQUES, LTD.

## THE BEER STEIN BOOK

by Gary Kirsner & Jim Gruhl
(ISBN: 0-9614130-3-4)

The most detailed book ever written about antique beer steins, with over 2400 steins illustrated, including 300 in color. A hardcover book of 416 pages, 9" x 12", including 32 color pages, it includes sections covering Faience, Glass, Character, Regimental, Stoneware, Pottery, Pewter, Porcelain, Mettlach, non-Mettlach etched, Military, Brewery, Post World War II, and Unusual Materials, including Silver, Ivory and Wood.

## THE METTLACH BOOK (Second Edition)

by Gary Kirsner
(ISBN: 0-9614130-1-8)

The Mettlach Book is a hardcover book of 351 pages, 9" x 12", with 16 pages in color in which over 2800 Mettlach items (50% are steins) are described and priced. Over 1500 of these items are illustrated, including 172 in color.

## GERMAN MILITARY STEINS, 1914-1945

by Gary Kirsner
(ISBN: 0-9614130-2-6)

A history of military steins and information about production is included in this 96 page, 6" x 9", softcover book. Two hundred and sixty-nine steins are illustrated, with descriptions and values.

See your local bookseller or write to:

**GLENTIQUES, LTD.   P.O. BOX 8807   CORAL SPRINGS, FL 33075
PHONE: 305-344-9856   FAX: 305-344-4421**